Modernis

Blackwell Introductions to Literature

This series sets out to provide concise and stimulating introductions to literary subjects. It offers books on major authors (from John Milton to James Joyce), as well as key periods and movements (from Old English literature to the contemporary). Coverage is also afforded to such specific topics as 'Arthurian Romance'. All are written by outstanding scholars as texts to inspire newcomers and others: non-specialists wishing to revisit a topic, or general readers. The prospective overall aim is to ground and prepare students and readers of whatever kind in their pursuit of wider reading.

Published

1. John Milton	Roy Flannagan
2. James Joyce	Michael Seidel
3. Chaucer and the Canterbury Tales	John Hirsh
4. Arthurian Romance	Derek Pearsall
5. Mark Twain	Stephen Railton
6. The Modern Novel	Jesse Matz
7. Old Norse-Icelandic Literature	Heather O'Donoghue
8. Old English Literature	Daniel Donoghue
9. Modernism	David Ayers

Modernism

A Short Introduction

David Ayers

Blackwell
Publishing

BLACKWELL PUBLISHING
350 Main Street, Malden, MA 02148-5020, USA
108 Cowley Road, Oxford OX4 1JF, UK
550 Swanston Street, Carlton, Victoria 3053, Australia

First published 2004 by Blackwell Publishing Ltd

Library of Congress Cataloging-in-Publication Data

Ayers, David, 1960–
Modernism : a short introduction / David Ayers.
   p. cm. – (Blackwell introductions to literature)
Includes bibliographical references (p.) and index.
ISBN 1-4051-0854-1 (hardcover : alk. paper) –
ISBN 1-4051-0853-3 (pbk. : alk. paper)
   1. English literature – 20th century – History and criticism.
2. Modernism (Literature) – Great Britain.   3. American literature – 20th
century – History and criticism.   4. Modernism (Literature) – United
States.   I. Title.   II. Series.

PR478.M6A98 2004
820.9'112–dc22
2003025564

A catalogue record for this title is available from the British Library.

Set in 10/13pt Meridian
by Graphicraft Limited, Hong Kong
Printed and bound in the United Kingdom
by T.J. International, Padstow, Cornwall

For further information on
Blackwell Publishing, visit our website:
http://www.blackwellpublishing.com

For Paul and Hazel

Contents

Acknowledgements

I would like to acknowledge the support of the School of English at Kent University in allowing me leave to write this book. The school has provided a valuable context for my work, and I thank the colleagues and students who have provided the environment in which I have been able to develop my thinking. Particular thanks are due to Jan Montefiore and David Herd of the Centre for Modern Poetry at Kent, and to students on the MA in modern poetry, who have contributed to the formation of many of the ideas in this book.

It has been my pleasure over the years to discuss modernism with a large number of scholars, established and otherwise, among whom I count many personal friends. Over the years, I have found among them as winning a combination of seriousness, commitment and geniality as I could have hoped to encounter, and I have constantly been motivated by their example in written discourse, in seminars and in personal conversation. Their scholarly and intellectual commitment is second to none, and has helped make the study of modernism a challenging, stimulating, purposeful and consistently pleasurable activity for all concerned.

Finally, I would like to thank my wife, Margaret, for all her understanding and support; my mother, who introduced me to Maggie Newbery's *Picking Up Threads*; and my brother Paul and his wife Hazel, to whom this book is dedicated.

The author and publisher also wish to thank the following for permission to use copyright material: 'Epigram' by H. D. (Hilda Doolittle), from *Collected Poems 1912–1944*, © 1982 by The Estate of Hilda Doolittle.

Introduction

A study of modernism might quite properly seek to spread its efforts across the literature, theatre, music and art of the first half of the twentieth century in Europe, America and beyond. Indeed it ought really to reach back into the nineteenth century, to the poetry of Baudelaire or the music theatre of Wagner. This modest book, intended for readers of literature in English, adopts a more restricted focus, limiting itself to a selection of the English-language literature of the same period, with a fairly marked bias towards the British side of the Atlantic.

This restriction of focus has the advantage that it has been possible to elaborate critical arguments and draw attention to nuances of interpretation and detail in a manner impossible in a study of broader scope. The aim is to help the user of this book to become an informed reader of modernism, and to grasp some aspects of the intellectual, historical and, in particular, *readerly* aspects of the reception of modernism. The coverage is inevitably partial, a feature augmented by the occasional introduction of what I believe to be illuminating sidelights, and the discussion ranges from almost microscopic detail to the broadest generalizations concerning the intellectual and cultural framework of the decades in question.

This approach is not arbitrary. I seek to give a flavour of the variety of materials and methods which are commonly brought to the study of modernism today. The following chapters are designed to be read as a series of interlinked essays. They are aimed at a user who has already embarked on the reading of modernism, and may already have encountered some of the more common claims and approaches made in the commentary on that literature. So I do not present a history, but try to give enough orienting material to give the novice a way in, while seeking to give a picture of possible responses to the field of modernist criticism as it is formed today. I do not provide the laborious mechanism of footnotes and critical references which are found in more scholarly studies, but I do provide chapter bibliographies which direct the reader to other studies I have consulted, where they will find reference to everything I mention and a good deal more beside.

The method is essayistic, then, but there is a connecting strand which runs through the book. The writers whom we call modernists had all asked themselves a simple and radical question: could art have a real social purpose? This question depended on another and more general one: was there any role for the individual in a society which was bourgeois, industrial, bureaucratically centralized, massified, and in the case of England overshadowed by the imperialist project of the Victorians? The questions were not new, but were present in some form in Victorian and before that Romantic literature. Indeed both of these questions were themselves intertwined in all of their aspects with the broadest general framework developed within the literature and thought of the Romantic period – the apparent loss of nature, or the separation of subject and object. The modernist writers who took these questions most seriously responded to them with literary innovations which seem at first glance to be technical experiments, but are in fact motivated by fundamental social questioning.

Modernism – especially if we include other languages and arts – presents a bewildering plurality of material, so much so that some have preferred to speak of modernisms in the plural. While such an emphasis on plurality is entirely warranted, I nevertheless believe that it is possible to develop an overarching narrative of the apparently fragmented arts of modernism. Broad themes about the nature of selfhood and consciousness, the autonomy of language, the role of art and of the artist, the nature of the industrial world, and the alienation of gendered existence form a set of concerns which manifest themselves across a range of works and authors. With this wide background of modernity in view, it is possible to tell a story which is accurate in outline and which enables the student of modernism to rise above the many local difficulties of modernist texts and see those texts in the global context which they share.

The first four chapters deal with poetry. Detailed remarks on Imagism in chapter 1 are followed by more abstract meditations on modernist reading in chapter 2, which takes Eliot's 'The Love Song of J. Alfred Prufrock' as its occasion. Chapter 3 juxtaposes Eliot's well-known long poem 'The Waste Land' with two less well-known sequences which are proving of increasing interest to critics: Nancy Cunard's *Parallax* and Mina Loy's 'Songs to Joannes'. In contrast to these works, chapter 4 concentrates on the work of Wallace Stevens, whose detailed attention to the poetic logic of the relationship of subject to object is the culmination of a certain modernist form of textual self-awareness.

The next four chapters turn to prose. Chapter 5 deals with Wyndham Lewis, whose vitriolic treatment of modernity is increasingly seen as central to this period. Chapter 6 attempts to bypass the complexity of *Ulysses* by drawing attention to the theme of love as the work's attempted response to a pessimistic vision of modernity. D. H. Lawrence is approached obliquely in chapter 7 via the topic of jazz, in an attempt to refresh the palate. In chapter 8, I tackle the inescapable subject of Virginia Woolf's politics, by providing a bit of context and suggesting that we should give careful definition to our sense of her feminism.

In the final chapters I present in outline two of the major theoretical influences which have formed part of the reception of modernist literature in recent years, and which underpin, in large part, what I have said in the preceding chapters. Chapter 9 concerns the Hegelian Marxism of Theodor Adorno and Walter Benjamin, whom I approach via Georg Lukács. Their analysis of modernity is now integral to informed readers of modernism, and I have identified some of the key issues which give shape to their thinking. Finally in chapter 10, I attempt something similar for Jacques Derrida, outlining the basic intellectual necessities which called for deconstruction and set it into effect in the context of modernist reading.

I have been very conscious, throughout, of the limitation of coverage, and even more so of the limitation of argumentative development, which space has imposed on this project. I have indeed made a selection of materials and set priorities, as I was obliged to do, and having tailored this book to a broad readership, I sincerely hope that no one will mistake omission for exclusion. In the same vein, by attempting to set down a palette of argumentative material which might bring these texts and issues to life, I am at times excruciatingly aware of the periodic loss of subtlety involved. Note that where I summarize, for example, a writer's view on the artist, and use 'he' rather than 'he or she', I am presenting views which I regard as definitely or probably gendered, and I do not wish to rewrite history by making any writer appear more egalitarian in temperament than seems to have been the case.

This is not a history of modernism, but a *critical introduction*. I hope that readers will find it provocative and a stimulus to further study and reflection. With good fortune, they may explain to me, in future years, exactly why my claims are so *wrong*. That, above all, is the nature of the dialogue we call *criticism*.

CHAPTER 1

H. D., Ezra Pound and Imagism

The poetic movement of Imagism is often the first glimpse that the general reader gains of the poetry of Ezra Pound. The short history of the Imagist movement occupies a key moment in Pound's career, providing important insights into a long and complex development. It also gives access to a series of other careers, English and American, which were temporarily brought together in an attempt to impose themselves on the literary world as the next big thing.

It is worth pausing over the notion of an artistic movement of any kind. In English letters, the notion of a movement which would announce itself through manifestos designed to shape audience taste was not a novelty. William Wordsworth and Samuel Taylor Coleridge attempted something similar in *Lyrical Ballads*, especially with the addition of the famous 1802 'Preface' which appears to us now as a permanent document of Romanticism. However, Wordsworth and Coleridge did not *call* themselves Romantics. Really, the notion of a group of artists announcing themselves to the world as a movement with a collective identity had come into fashion again in the first decade of the twentieth century, as various avant-gardes in the different arts sought identification for their particular style, or combined with other arts to insist on a collective identity. Italian Futurism was perhaps the most recent movement to impact on England in the early 1910s, offering a brash, anti-bourgeois modernism, an alliance of all the arts, and a commitment to creating an art of modernism which looked forward to an increasingly industrialized world. Futurism had the advantage of a very noticeable leader and theorist in the person of the abrasive and outspoken F. T. Marinetti, who took a delight in provoking an audience and confronting received notions about the proper nature of art and audience.

Imagism was first given shape in 1912, and kept going in a series of Imagist anthologies until 1917. Ezra Pound himself, though substantially the creator of the movement, jumped ship and aligned himself with Wyndham Lewis's Vorticism in 1914, probably because Vorticism offered the seduction of an alliance between painting, sculpture and literature, and because Lewis's movement more resembled Futurism in its confrontational approach to existing aesthetic practices and to what were perceived as being the sedentary bourgeois tastes dominating all of artistic production and consumption. Imagism as a literary movement did not adopt the global and confrontational stance of Futurism. Nevertheless it was an umbrella for an interesting range of writers, and the occasion of an important moment of literary theorization.

The term 'Imagist' was conjured by Ezra Pound to characterize the style of recent work by his friends and collaborators, the American Hilda Doolittle (H. D.) and the Englishman Richard Aldington. Pound sent three poems each by H. D. and Aldington to Harriet Monroe, editor of the Chicago-based journal *Poetry*. Pound wrote to Monroe: 'This is the sort of American stuff that I can show here in Paris without its being ridiculed. Objective – no slither; direct – no excessive use of adjectives; no metaphors that won't permit examination. It's straight talk, straight as the Greek!'[1] Pound would reformulate and develop this manifesto on several subsequent occasions, but in essence all of the central claims are in place. Of course it is not all American, though this claim is not only there for Monroe's benefit. Imagism aims to bring modern speech into poetry, and rejects the English late Victorian style which it considers has become verbose. The comparison with the Greek is very important. Aldington and H. D. shared an interest in classical poetry, and they found in Greek poetry – especially the surviving fragments of the Lesbian poetess Sappho – a directness which they felt had no equal in contemporary modes of writing in English. They sought to recreate such writing for themselves as the basis of a new modern idiom, and in doing so helped provide the basis for a key element in English modernism – neo-classicism. 'Classicism' became the favoured term behind which such anti-Romantics as T. S. Eliot, Pound and Lewis would organize their projects. It later came to take on a whole swathe of political and cultural meanings, but in its aesthetic dimension the point of reference is always Romanticism. These writers believed that Romantic art was over-subjective, and argued for a renewed emphasis on the object-like nature of the art-work. The intellectual ramification for this came from the poet F. S. Flint and the philosopher T. E. Hulme (both contributors to the weekly magazine *New Age*), and is reflected in such literary critical notions as the 'objective correlative' briefly expounded by Eliot in his essay on Hamlet;[2] Pound, H. D. and Aldington gave the movement an aesthetic reality which in its sheer delicacy seems surprisingly different in scale to the theorization of 'classicism' which eventually followed.

One of the Imagist poems first published in *Poetry* and subsequently in the first Imagist anthology was H. D.'s 'Epigram'. The poem demonstrates several interests of the Imagists, and establishes not least that the notion of the 'image' does not refer simply to the visual image. The poem is an adaptation of a Greek epigram of unknown authorship:

> The golden one is gone from the banquets;
> She, beloved of Atimetus,
> The swallow, the bright Homonoea;
> Gone the dear chatterer.[3]

H. D.'s method is best understood with reference to the original from which she is working. This is an epitaph which appears in the *Greek Anthology*, and which can be found as epigram no. XLVI in the 'Epitaphs' section of J. W. Mackail's *Select Epigrams from the Greek Anthology* (1907). This tiny volume, which does not include translations, is itself almost a model for the Imagist anthologies, presenting the most gracefully concise writing to be found in ancient Greek literature. The original occupies six lines, and can be found in translation in this form:

'On Claudia Homonoea'
Author Unknown

I Homonoea, who was far clearer-voiced than the Sirens, I who was more golden than the Cyprian herself at revellings and feasts, I the chattering bright swallow lie here, leaving tears to Atimetus, to whom

I was dear from girlhood; but unforeseen fate scattered all that great affection.[4]

We might also set this against the version of this poem which H. D.'s editor includes in her *Collected Poems* of 1983. It features an extra line which the author had deleted before publication:

> The golden one is gone from the banquets;
> She, beloved of Atimetus,
> The swallow, the bright Homonoea;
> Gone the dear chatterer;
> Death succeeds Atimetus.[5]

H. D.'s version is more economical, more oblique, and more neutral in tone than the literal translation. She is not simply rendering the Greek epigram, but transforming it into an idiom which is, if possible, even more epigrammatic. The content of the original is certainly simplified and reduced, and this is done with a view to removing its overt emotion. The translation exploits the pathos of the dead speaking her own epitaph, but H. D.'s version, in which the first person has disappeared, is in this respect closer to the original. The classical references in the original (to the Sirens, Bacchus and Aphrodite) have been removed, to avoid a deadening 'classicizing' effect, with only the names of the lovers remaining. The fifth and unpublished line is an attempt to avert direct emotion with a figure that requires unpacking, condensing as it does the metaphor of death succeeding Atimetus as the lover of Homonoea. This notion was H. D.'s own and does not appear in the original, and was probably excluded not because the idea is a bad one, but because the repetition of Atimetus is clumsy (it is enough to give his name once), and since Homonoea has already twice been said to be 'gone' it seems unnecessary to point out that she is dead. In fact, the repetition of 'gone' is itself redundant and ought, by the canons of Imagism – to 'use no unnecessary word' – to have been eliminated.

H. D.'s poem is not a translation, but a loose version in which aesthetic goals related to the ideals of the Greek epigram are reconfigured as a modern poetics which specifically seeks to substitute a laconic detachment for what was perceived as the emotional effusiveness of the late Victorian poets. In fact, there are few Imagist poems which really fulfil the criteria of Imagism. Aldington's 'To a Greek Marble',[6] though a featured work of Imagism, is littered with 'thee', 'thou' and 'thy', runs for 23 lines, and seeks to evoke pathos too directly. Imagism is interesting not so much for the range of work which it produced as for the intentions which shaped it and for its theoretical underpinning, which Pound, in particular, developed into a whole poetics that in a variety of forms would buttress the work which occupied him for the whole of his writing life from 1917 onwards – *The Cantos*.

Like H. D., Pound at this time was seeking to create a modern mode of writing which would provide a flexible alternative to the Victorian mode, and satisfy a new aesthetic criterion based not on emotional indulgence but on the precision of the practice of writing itself. Pound pursued this goal over a number of years with incredible single-mindedness. In doing so he developed not one but many ways of writing a modern poem, and the extent of his achievement and of his art should be lost on no one – though Pound was evidently so successful, and so influential on the major practitioners of poetry, that aspects of his art might be invisible to first-time readers.

Pound's 'The Return' is a fully realized exercise in the kind of free verse tempered by metrical precision that he made into the centrepiece of his art. This poem is ostensibly about hunters returning to a hunt in which they once participated gloriously, but who now are tentative in their approach, perhaps wary of trying their powers once again. The content is given a classical air, but there is no reference to any specific and ready-made mythological situation. The situation has no explanation outside the poem, as if the idea were to evoke an atmosphere without reliance on any external scenario. Moreover, the uncertainty of the returning hunters is matched by the uncertainty of the reader who tries – and fails – to recognize a familiar situation in this poem. It is above all the sense of uncertain motion that Pound tries to create – the writing is much more about the mode and movement of the poem than about any supposed content:

> See, they return; ah, see the tentative
> Movements, and the slow feet,
> The trouble in the pace and the uncertain
> Wavering![7]

The reference to 'feet' reminds us that technique is an abiding concern of Pound's. Here, in a *tour de force* of prosodic technique, Pound demonstrates that the organization of the poetic foot – the basic unit of verse – must be as rigorous in the context of free verse as it is in that of formal verse. The metric organization in free verse is given not by the set of demands of any adopted verse pattern, but by the content itself, so that the very movement of the verse will suggest a kind of concrete content. In this poem, it is the shape of a stumbling, tentative motion, along with a slow gaining of confidence, which the verse form musically imitates and embodies. As Pound explained:

> I believe in an ultimate and absolute rhythm as I believe in an absolute symbol or metaphor. The perception of the intellect is given in the word, that of the emotions in the cadence. [. . .] The rhythm of any poetic line corresponds to emotion. It is the poet's business that this correspondence be exact, i.e., that it be the emotion which surrounds the thought expressed.[8]

One aspect of this passage is that it reveals the almost mystical importance that Pound gave to the organization of sound in poetry. He called this 'MELOPOEIA, wherein the words are charged, over and above their plain meaning, with some musical property, which directs the bearing or trend of that meaning'.[9] Note that Pound does not merely celebrate the mellifluousness of wonderful-sounding poetry – far from it. His notion is that the sound of verse corresponds to a certain type of meaning quite as definitely as does its semantic content. On the one hand, a work like 'The Return' is a dazzling exercise in rendering a mood as much or more in terms of organization of sound as in terms of the elusive content. Here we see Pound the great virtuoso at work. On the other hand, what we also see at play is an aspect of his work which more recent and theoretically inflected critics have fastened on to – a theoretical insistence on a kind of absolute meaning, which adopts various forms throughout Pound's career, but is a relative constant and is viewed suspiciously by modern readers brought up on the theory of the differential displacement of meaning, which (as we shall see later) Jacques Derrida has extracted from the work of the linguist Ferdinand de Saussure. There are clear extrinsic reasons, too, to regard Pound's theories of meaning as tending to an authoritarian closure – his later advocacy of Mussolini and his virulent anti-Semitism lead us to examine his theories of poetic language with a sceptical eye.

In some sense we have two Pounds: on the one hand, one of the principal inventors of modern poetry, who throughout his career (and not merely in his early years) created novel modes of poetic writing and led the way in showing others how many things modern poetry could be; on the other hand, a political undesirable, whose attempts to theorize his art and to give it a social role are too involved with his reprehensible anti-Semitic theory – for Pound was not simply a bigot or racist but a committed anti-Semitic *theorist*.

I would like to stay with Pound the technician for a moment, although in the context of poetry 'technique' is not an adequate term. 'Technique' implies that poetry might have a 'substance' which precedes expression, even, a general content already given a broadly literary form; 'technique', this notion suggests, is merely the finishing process in which details of no interest to the consumer are attended to, the behind-the-scenes mechanics of which only the engineer need be aware. It should hardly need saying that 'technique' goes to the heart of the mode of being of poetry – technique '*is*' what poetry '*is*', its substance as an object and activity, not merely its manner of presenting some other substance. Pound's capacity for creating new poetic modes testifies to a real hunger for writing as an art, not simply a means to some end, even if his work eventually became involved in a general crisis for the notion of the artist.

In the same, often cited passage in which he talks about 'melopoeia', Pound also discusses 'logopoeia', a term which he says refers to 'the dance of the intellect among words', adding that 'it employs words not only for their direct meaning, but it takes count in a special way of habits of usage, of the context we *expect* to find with the word, its usual concomitants, of its known acceptances, and of ironical play. [. . .] It is the latest come, and perhaps most tricky and undependable mode.'[10] This is a condensed characterization of the modern mode of writing, which might include the laconic speech of Imagism and the irony of Eliot's 'Prufrock', as well as some of Pound's most remarkable early writing. Here, Pound succinctly characterizes the self-conscious modernist mode of working with different discursive sources to produce a complex 'world', and the particular pleasure of playful interaction which accompanies this art of discursive mixing. Yet even in these early formulations, there is a crisis developing for

Pound, concerning the purpose and meaning of the writer as artist, and of writing as art.

Pound was aware of the forces shaping this dilemma because, in a literary London newly aware of continental art movements, the pressures on the notion of 'art' were visibly mounting. His poem 'Les Millwin' is a wry exercise in his own art, which also serves as a satirical documentation of the confrontation between the stance of aestheticism of the 1890s and the incoming Futurist attitude to art. It is characterized as a juxtaposition of the anaemic, wealthy Millwins (whose surname, in the title of the poem, is absurdly offset by the French 'les') and the robust art students from the Slade School (where Wyndham Lewis studied). The setting is a performance by Diaghilev's Russian Ballet, the height of fashion at that time. In the audience are the young Millwin family, lying on the seats 'like so many unused boas', and the art students, a 'rigorous deputation from "Slade"' who hold aloft their 'fore-arms / crossed in great futuristic X's'. The approach of the poem is to create an image as object-like as possible, avoiding comment and concluding only with two dry lines:

> Let us therefore mention the fact,
> For it seems to us worthy of record.[11]

Pound satirically objectifies both sides in the imaginary juxtaposition, then withdraws from any further authorial comment or other explanation of the material.

The art of creating an object-like structure in words was taken virtually to its limit in this famous poem:

> *In a Station of the Metro*
>
> The apparition of these faces in the crowd:
> Petals, on a wet, black bough.[12]

Perhaps remarkably, considering the brevity of the poem, there are various versions of the text, and readers will excuse the fact that I have opted for the version contained in Pound's 1914 essay 'Vorticism', since it is this extended essay which furnishes the theoretical commentary on language which, in its various forms, Pound developed as an increasingly central component of his subsequent work.

The poem itself perhaps requires little commentary. Like a Romantic lyric, it attempts to capture a moment of heightened aesthetic awareness, but it does so with a pronounced economy of means. There is no 'poet' present, no 'I', not even a main verb. Instead there is just a location given, in the title, an image of faces briefly evoked, and, by means of a juxtaposition, a further image introduced which serves as a simile or analogue of the first. Although Pound remarks in his commentary on this poem that 'it is meaningless unless one has drifted into a certain vein of thought' (p. 89), in fact the opposite could be asserted: that such a work demands very little in the way of emotional assent or intellectual participation from the reader. It is what it is: a juxtaposition of images of the starkest kind. While we can adduce a certain type of aesthetic emotion on the part of the poet whom we imagine undergoing this experience in the Parisian Metro, this remains not only understated but unstated, a mere possibility left, undiscussed, in the background.

The reader of 'In a Station of the Metro' *may* of course generate a whole series of readings of this work, concerned with the city, the juxtaposition of nature and society, the underground Metro as a modern hell, the transitory and the permanent – thematically, there is a great deal here, even if materially there is not. Pound, shifting his allegiance from the Imagism which he had helped initiate, but which now seemed to him perhaps precious or tame, adopts the dynamic insistence of his new ally Wyndham Lewis, explaining that: 'The image is not an idea. It is a radiant node or cluster; it is what I can, and must perforce, call a VORTEX, from which, and through which, and into which, ideas are constantly rushing' (p. 92). In describing this 'rush' of ideas, Pound seeks to place the thinking outside the poem rather than within it – meanings are to be adduced rather than stated. However, as well as setting out an aesthetic manifesto, Pound begins to theorize the nature and status of poetic language. He will eventually move on from this to theorize language itself. Pound followed the tenets of post-Impressionist art in declaring that the Imagist poem was a matter of a purely formal arrangement. He compares the Imagist poem to an algebraic equation, 'not something about *a*, *b*, and *c*, having something to do with form, but about *sea*, *cliffs*, *night*, having something to do with mood' (p. 92). In tandem with this, he expresses a distrust of what he calls 'rhetoric' in language, in terms which suggest not simply an aesthetic hostility towards redundant words as used in poetry, but a doubt about the authenticity of words which can drift away from any secure meaning. On the one hand, by insisting that a composition in words can be as object-like as a sculpture, Pound makes an interesting assertion about the possible affinity of a linguistic and non-linguistic art-work, a comparison which is open to question but seems mostly stimulating and potentially productive. On the other hand, he opens the way to an insistence that words must be immediate and objective in their meaning, something problematic for language, which achieves its effects over time and can only ever approach, rather than assimilate, its object. Pound hopes to insist on a kind of immediate correspondence between word and thing. For this reason he advances the Chinese ideogram as a model for poetry. In this, he followed the scholar Ernest Fenollosa, whose book *The Chinese Written Character as a Medium for Poetry* Pound edited and brought to press. This book emphasized that the Chinese ideogram was, in its origin, pictorial in nature, and that therefore it offered a more direct mode of communication than Western phonetic script. Fenollosa wrote: 'Chinese poetry [. . .] speaks at once with the vividness of painting, and with the mobility of sounds. It is, in some sense, more objective than either, more dramatic. In reading Chinese we do not seem to be juggling mental counters, but to be watching *things* work out their own fate.'[13]

In Pound's art there is, almost paradoxically, a distrust of language, especially of writing, which extended into a similar distrust of money. Money, like language, circulates with no real certainty that the object which it 'represents' will ever be restored. Like language, money is peculiarly groundless. Pound's long anti-Semitic campaign in his work takes root in his developing theory, throughout the later 1920s and 1930s, that corruption of the meaning of words and corruption of the value of money could be blamed on Jews.

How possible is it to read the early poetry of Pound without making mental reference to the politics he developed? One reason that we cannot in any simple fashion separate the two is the manner in which the Imagist method was transformed and extended throughout the *Cantos*. In 1948 Pound published a volume called *The Pisan Cantos*. This series of works had been written in Pisa in 1945, when Pound was under arrest for treason by US forces. At one point held on death row, later moved on account of his age (he was 60), these were unpromising circumstances for the composition of a major masterpiece. Not only that, the matter of the *Pisan Cantos* was a lament for the defeat of Mussolini and Italian Fascism, a similarly unpromising matter as far as many English-speaking readers might have been concerned at that time. Yet the *Pisan Cantos* are a remarkable work which set a new standard in modern poetry. Pound finds an idiom, based on the brevity, allusiveness, and juxtapositions of Imagism, that is a perfect vehicle for a review of his own life and untimely entry into history. The fragments which make up these Cantos concern the whole of his thought, the people he has known, the art he has loved and the places he has visited, all combined in a lament which is also an aggressive defiance of the forces that have eclipsed the developing experiment in social organization which (as Pound saw it) the defeat of Italy had cruelly ended. The plangent tones in which he insists that his idea of an ideal state can be preserved in his mind, even if the attempt to realize it has been destroyed, is presented in terms of great grace and economy, juxtaposing the personal and the cultural in an idiom which seems to come easily yet which is hard won. In dialogue with an absent friend, Pound writes: 'yet say this to the Possum: a bang, not a whimper, / with a bang not with a whimper'. Pound rebukes Eliot (the Possum) for the quiescence of his poem 'The Hollow Men', which ends 'not with a bang but a whimper'. Pound ends, yes, defiantly lamenting the execution of Mussolini by Italian partisans in the closing stage of the war, but also with a work which is a defiant *tour de force* that, whether we choose to attend to it or not, is the culmination of Imagism and one of the defining works of modernist poetry.

CHAPTER 2

T. S. Eliot and Modernist Reading

Pound and the Imagists, in offering an object-like poetry, presented their readers with the relatively modest challenges of wit and the epigram. The poetry of T. S. Eliot tests readers and commentators more robustly, in that its use of words implies an aesthetic of reading which goes beyond the simply stated goal of Imagist objectivity. While Pound's essays, in particular, supply an adequate basis for the analysis of Imagism, Eliot's works are designed to satisfy more complex goals, and his numerous literary and theoretical essays offer only fragmentary support to the theorization of his poetry. Imagism can, in a more or less satisfactory way, be returned to a framing history. It is harder to give an account of Eliot's work from the outside, one which might supply the explanation, say that which the work does not say (which, once said, will complete it), make clear what was obscure. The transparency of Imagism may be more apparent than real, since the real difficulty which any literary artefact presents is that, while it consists of words, it makes no claims. Eliot's poetry presents its readers with an acute question of literary interpretation: how far is it possible to render transparent and available to rational understanding a linguistic object which, though it contains numerous statements, makes no rational claims?

Every literary text provokes these questions: Eliot's do so in the most self-conscious fashion of any modernist writer. Such questions take a general form which they have often been given: what is the function of criticism? Does criticism add to or replace the original text, grafting layer after layer of words upon the original words? Or does criticism prepare and enlighten the reader, who can thereafter return to the text for a more fulfilling, but mute, experience of reading the original? Is the point to arrive at a discursive consensus regarding the meaning-generating capacity of the text, or is the point to remove extraneous meanings and be true to the text?

Such questions – and they have been endlessly elaborated in literary critical discourse – might be provoked by any text, and they are certainly provoked by Eliot's writing. As well as having a general dimension, however, such questions must also be asked of any specific text. What is the criticism of any particular text? What does this particular piece of writing call for? What features of this particular text and its particular mode of presentation might call for a certain type of commentary which another text – another literary or non-literary text – does not summon? In what way is this text *this* text, and what does that imply for commentary?

Posed in this fashion, such questions seem, paradoxically, reassuring. The questions themselves imply a broad movement of open-ended questioning, as if *these questions* had themselves become the substance of any critical operation. Who reads and why? Who says what about a text? When, where and why do they say it? These questions are, generally, materialist questions. They are questions about what social interest is at play in a text. Is a text propagated by a social elite, made available only to the educated, designed to prop up or endorse existing social authority? Or is the text produced by an excluded individual, propagated by an excluded group, designed to subvert existing social authority? Marxist, feminist and postcolonial criticism are only three of the critical modes which ask and answer such questions. In large part, this is a question of the social situation of a text, with regard to readership, distribution, reception.

In contrast to those modes which seek to locate a text at a historical and social nexus are those modes of commentary which ask quite different questions. How does a text mean? What, in a text, is irreducible to history, society? How far do problems of understanding the nature of textuality itself riddle or ruin any attempt to posit the meaning of a text which functions merely as a provocative cipher, the already-past occasion for endless, disseminative works of commentary, which never restore the text, but further multiply its already irrecuperable plurality? This is the stance of the traditions of close reading and Anglo-American deconstruction.

Each set of questions, as I have already suggested, is paradoxically reassuring. On the one hand, the questions themselves seem on the face of it potentially radical and far reaching. On the other, they are as reassuring as a set of introductory notes for students, because once posed they seem negotiable. Yes, they are questions. In the first case they appear to be answerable by a mixture of historically solid research and theoretically informed speculation (about the nature of the modern subject in terms of gender, ethnicity, sexuality and class). The speculative element purports to theorize the nature of alienation in modern society – for example, the art-work can be described as a commodity in terms that draw on Karl Marx's theory of the commodity in *Capital*, itself an attempt to theorize the nature of alienation under the modern social formation of capitalism. Such speculative elements can be both extremely rigorous and highly problematic – the influential work of Judith Butler on sexuality and gender is a case in point. However, the speculation itself seems to lack danger – is in fact the occasion of at least delight (in the possible intricacy of thinking) and perhaps solidarity (in the politics of self-articulation and liberation). History is fact, and always reassuring; speculation is well-intentioned, and unlikely ever to result in an increase in alienation – it is unlikely to make matters worse, in other words, and can be safely indulged.

The reassurance which such modes of *questioning* supply is that of bringing an art-work under textual control, bringing it to reason even when what reason produces is only a question, an uncertainty, a carefully controlled oscillation. As I have suggested, the whole process is delightful, and we should not for one moment renounce delight. Yet our impression is less and less that we are involved in some process through which we have grown as readers and transcended, incorporated, and either mastered our text or identified ourselves with its carefully generated moment of loss of mastery over its own 'meaning', a meaning which is in any case no longer its 'own'. Our impression is increasingly that we are part of a slow and inexorable social machinery which in one way or another is bringing everything under critical control.

Why should we worry? Maybe we should not. But, if we find ourselves worrying, *how*, or on what terms, might we do so? The first and most obvious temptation is to make a claim for reading, for the basic moments which just plain *reading* a text can bring – the pure unmediated *affectivity* of a text. A text *moves* us, it makes claim to our *sympathy*, it provides us with *identification*, we feel *empathy* or *disgust* or

– whatever. Literary commentary often makes recourse to analogies with music when it is unable to theorize itself, and in this case the analogy is with the *blues*, the African American music of the Mississippi Delta renowned for its supposedly raw expressiveness, its untutored nature, its ability to voice collective pleasure and pain.

Yet even as we make recourse to affectivity – even where we have the apparent legitimacy of the blues as an analogy for our claims – suspicion falls heavily on the notion of an experience of language which is somehow in itself non-linguistic. We can experience the thrill or terror of the sea falling over us – if we can borrow the sea, here, temporarily, from Prufrock – but that is not a knowledge of the sea and it is not something within language. It is a kind of non-linguistic bodily experience. How then can we have an experience of language, and how do we rationalize the basis of that experience? Even in the case of the sea falling over us, our experience depends on what we anticipate and on what we remember. What appears at first to be a bodily 'experience' is one that we know through the protentive and retentive operations of the mind, one that is put into relation with other experiences, something that is not a true singularity at all. Yet as modernist writing will often insist – Virginia Woolf spoke of 'moments of being' – the moment of experience will always give the powerful impression of its immediacy, its uniqueness, its absolute sensory particularity, even though we *know* that as a moment it exists for us only in relation to other moments. Indeed, each moment of being might be broken down into an ensemble of discrete moments; so the experience of the wave falling over us consists of a manifold visual impression, a multitudinous aural impression, and a complex and differentiated physical impact on our body, to say nothing of the taste as the water goes up our nose and into our mouth. So even what we might consider to be a unitary 'moment' or 'experience' consists of many moments, none of which we can easily isolate as they present almost simultaneously. The 'moment' is in fact a complex synthesis of differentiated sense impressions, which are in part grasped by the mind, giving an impression of unity, and in large part overwhelm the mind, giving an impression of pure excess, an impossibility of really and fully knowing what constitutes the event of the 'moment', an inability on our part to be fully present at that which we experience, or properly to bring it to mind afterwards. Eliot, who muses on the temporal nature of experience throughout his poetry, expresses this gnomically: 'We had the experience but missed the meaning' (*Four Quartets*, 'The Dry Salvages').

So if it is hard to experience a single apparently sensuous 'moment' (and even more difficult to draw together the imperfect recollection of innumerable such moments in order to grasp a 'lifetime of experience'), how much harder must it be to think of *reading* as an experience. We have said that some modes of literary criticism seek to turn the object-text into knowledge by asking questions of it and producing discourse about it. In such forms of criticism the critical act itself becomes a kind of meta-narrative or master text which contains, controls and, in effect, supplants the object-text, which becomes an object of knowledge and is assigned its place in the collective mind of the world. In contrast with those approaches, we have asked what it means to have an experience of a text which might *not* take the form of the translation of that text into something else. In the process of pursuing this inquiry, we have already seen that the idea of an immediate experience of anything at all is a notion fraught with complexity and unsustainable without considerable modification. We have mentioned in passing that modernists such as Woolf and Eliot are already aware of the problems attached to the idea of a 'moment' of experience, already alerting us to the fact that this problem is one already bodied forth in the texts we are attempting to read, and is not one that supervenes on them retrospectively from the outside, so to speak. It will be no surprise then that this final issue – the notion of 'experiencing' a text in the movement of reading it – is also one of which modernist texts seem to be aware.

What do we experience when we read and how do we communicate or share that experience? What does it even mean to consider reading as an experience? Immanuel Kant, who treated the issue of aesthetic experience in general in his *Critique of Judgement* (see below, chapter 10), decreed that the aesthetic was non-conceptual, a notion that was taken up in German Romantic thought and which became the basis for some thinkers to consider the aesthetic as the mode in which nature and mind were united. Yet even Kant's troubling and productive insight about the aesthetic in general is not enough to figure the problems incumbent on considering the literary artefact as an aesthetic one, because the literary artefact is linguistic and is therefore already conceptual, already coded, not an immediate experience at all.

While we might well feel that a painting or a piece of music can fall over us non-conceptually, as the wave of the sea fell over us in our example, it is impossible to think that a text – even a literary text – can fall over us preconceptually in the same manner. Words are not experiences. Literature often, but not always, highlights the sensuous quality of the sound of words; these effects are analysed under the rubric 'verse'. Poetry in particular will also highlight the physical dimension of words inasmuch as they are traces arranged on a page. Occasionally poetry will arrange words pictorially or graphically – the Futurist poet F. T. Marinetti produced images of words arranged pictorially, and Ezra Pound endorsed a claim that the Chinese written character was in itself an ideal medium for poetry since it incorporated stylized pictorial elements in the very form of the writing. Whatever sensuous element the physical signifiers might have, and whatever means writing might employ to highlight the sensuous element and to make it a content of the art-work, it is seemingly inescapable that writing consists of signification, of signs that in some fashion stand for *something else*, refer to some experience or some fact according to an at least partially common code.

If writing refers to experience, then, how can reading itself be an experience? How can reading be 'of the moment'? As opposed to the attempt to elaborate on or explicate a linguistic artefact by the production of more language, there have been occasional attempts to approach the question about how the subject is present to the text, and the text to the subject, through a reflection on the nature of language not as speaking, but as hearing. These can only be mentioned briefly here. They include Martin Heidegger's reflections on poetry and language which employed the following formulation: 'Language speaks. Man speaks in that he responds to language. This responding is a hearing. It hears because it listens to the command of stillness.'[1] In an entirely different inflection, Jacques Lacan emphasizes that the subject is constructed by signification, but only via a process in which signification emerges elsewhere: 'The subject is born in so far as the signifier emerges in the field of the Other. But, by this very fact, this subject – which, was previously nothing if not a subject coming into being – solidifies into a signifier.'[2] In the field of criticism, the critic and educator F. R. Leavis was well known for his approach of attempting to induct his students into a subjective knowledge of texts by outlining claims about the effect of a text and confronting them with the question, 'This is so, isn't it?' Though it can easily be construed as an authoritarian gesture designed to bully assent from students, Leavis was approaching the difficult task of developing students as readers or receivers of language, and attempting to go beyond the question of simply knowing-what-to-say about a text.

I merely want to mention these inherently complicated alternative views here as different takes on the issue of hearing a text rather than knowing or commenting on it. I should say that these alternatives, from philosophy, psychoanalysis and literary theory, while not as completely isolated from each other as their apparently distinct disciplinary origins might seem to suggest, all stem from very different intellectual trajectories. They have in common the notion of language as a thing heard rather than a thing produced, and this is an idea of which modernism is aware. Samuel Beckett's work can be understood as an extension or making explicit of certain structural issues about the nature of language and subjectivity which are already present in earlier modernist texts. The subject as a listener to a voice which comes from another place is a favoured topic of Beckett's: he treats it in his play *Krapp's Last Tape*, in which an aged protagonist listens to taped diaries made by himself as a young man, and in *Not I*, a play which features a disembodied mouth addressing a silent shrouded figure that periodically shrugs, helplessly.

We began with a question for criticism about what it means to hear poetry mutely as opposed to saying something about it, and we have begun to say that the nature of saying/hearing is inscribed in modernist writing. If we add to this (a) that a heard voice is one heard both by the producer of the voice and by the hearer, and (b) that the concept of a heard 'voice' is itself a concept used to interpret or decipher a written text, then we are ready to begin reading 'The Love Song of J. Alfred Prufrock'.[3]

Referring to the fact that the name Prufrock appears only in the title of the poem, the critic Hugh Kenner famously commented that 'J. Alfred Prufrock is a name plus a Voice', and rightly argued that Prufrock is not a 'character' such as is found in one of the dramatic monologues of Tennyson or Browning.[4] Let us take the second part of this first. The dramatic monologue, such as Tennyson's 'Simeon Stylites' or Browning's 'My Last Duchess', is an attempt to encapsulate a character and situation in a manner reminiscent of the characteristic monologue of a Shakespeare play – the moment in which the essence of a character and his or her situation is summed up. Not accidentally, Prufrock makes glancing reference to Hamlet, whose speech 'To be or not to be' is one of the most typical and well known in this regard. The dramatic monologue as found in Tennyson and Browning did treat themes that were close to the poets themselves – typically the relationship between art and power – and were in a fashion veiled or highly mediated reflections on the situation of the poet. Nevertheless, the mode was dramatic, in that the reader is obliged to reconstruct the character and the implied situation to understand them, and part of the point of such works is that they seem to offer a glimpse into an entirely other world. Eliot's 'Prufrock' is not dissimilar to these dramatic monologues, but the dramatic situation is much harder to reconstruct, and there is a strong sense of the reader being plunged into an obscure involvement with the 'character' of Prufrock, rather than being able to hold him at a distance as if he were a character in a drama, most definitely not the poet, and most definitely not *us*, certainly not *me*. Pound, close to Eliot in many ways, but never really coming from the same position, praised 'Prufrock' as a satire. This seems very wrong, as if Eliot's idea had been simply to hold up a figure for mockery. Yet Prufrock invites mockery.

So in response to the model of Prufrock as a 'character' conveyed in the medium of verse, we must begin to conclude that 'verse' – perhaps just language – is brought to the fore in a process which renders inadequate that character exposition of the kind we might engage in when analysing a 'speech' of Hamlet in a school exercise. We have already emphasized 'voice' and 'speech' here in such a way as to suggest that these apparently innocuous terms in fact embody ideas, and to imply further that the ideas which they incorporate are to be regarded with some suspicion; hence the 'scare quotes'. If Prufrock is said to be a 'name' and a 'voice', it is precisely in order to unsettle each of these notions. In relation to the 'name', we can say straightforwardly that the proper name of a person, while it points to their body and soul, cannot truly present, represent, embody the whole of that person, and it is unproblematic to see that this issue of making oneself present, of being present to others, is a central concern of the poem. The thematization of the name, which is confirmed by the very name under which Prufrock marches, is elaborated throughout the reading of the poem through the querying, or better, simply *unsettling* of the notion of voice.

To call 'voice' a notion is already to go too far. In the context of the person, the voice is the speech of the person. In relation to poetry, 'voice' is extended to include the cadences, phrasing, sound, almost the very signature of the poet writing in a particular, individualized style. In relation to listening in general, we tend to suppose that when a person speaks, what we hear comes from a single entity, a single psyche or mind. In fact the very basis of listening seems to be that we reconstruct what we hear as if it proceed from a single intention. In the context of poetry, we audit a poet's style as if it came from a single intention, as if style were the extension or expression of the inner essence of the poet. Pound considered the search for a poetic style to be a quest for sincerity. The exact cadences of a poem (let alone the particular words chosen), its particular organization of sound, should be a direct register of an authentic experience, some-thing that could only be communicated in an entirely individual idiom. 'Prufrock' seems to take the opposite tack.

From the French poet Jules Laforgue, Eliot had learnt the lesson of irony, the lesson that a writer could stand above style, be outside and superior to it, manipulate it and refuse self-expression through it. This notion of ironic distance, and of style as the manipulation of possible ways of speaking, informs Eliot's celebrated notion of 'impersonality' in poetry. As he expressed this in his often quoted essay 'Tradition and the Individual Talent': 'The progress of an artist is a continual self-sacrifice, a continual extinction of personality.'[5] Eliot is discussing tradition, and resisting the Romantic notion that poetry is a matter of self-expression:

> There are many people who appreciate the expression of sincere emotion in verse, and there is a smaller number of people who can appreciate technical excellence. But very few know when there is an expression of *significant* emotion, emotion which has its life in the poem and not in the history of the poet. The emotion of art is impersonal. And the poet cannot reach this impersonality without surrendering himself wholly to the work to be done.[6]

However, this seemingly 'classical' stance conceals that Eliot's poetry actually always deals with the problem of self-expression and related problems about poetic voice, identity and consciousness.

The first line of 'The Love Song of J. Alfred Prufrock' – 'Let us go then, you and I' – concisely plunges the reader into questions of text and voice. However, it is not enough to call these 'questions', since for the reader they do not take the form of questions, but of a certain responsibility, an appeal or call which must be responded to by reading. In one respect, of course, this is a dramatic form. Like the speaker of Browning's 'My Last Duchess', the speaker of the poem attempts to take a listener into his confidence. The confidence may be a burdensome one since, as the epigraph from Dante implies, this may be a confession of sin. In both Browning and Dante there is a very clear dramatic situation, but here neither the contours of the speaker 'I' nor those of the addressee 'you' are clearly marked.

We could view this introductory line formally, and say that it is about the pronoun – I, you – and about the pronominal position. What makes a person 'I' or 'you' is not the given identity of the person in herself or himself. It is a relation in which the other is acknowledged as an object, a not-I, and the self is acknowledged not merely as a subject but as an object for others. Moreover, the second person pronoun – the 'you' – does not simply acknowledge the other as an other – a he or she – but also attempts to bring that other into relation with the self. So the 'you and I' of this first line is an attempted seduction, an endeavour to gain the complicity of the other, to bring that other into relation with the self on terms which the self would like to be able to control. It is a seduction and a power relationship.

We can go further and say that this seduction harnesses a complex feature of language. On the one hand, the 'I' might seem to be 'in here', the other 'you' somewhere 'over there'. But at the point where these two pronouns are presented in language – the only point, of course, where they can actually appear – they are brought into relation in the same medium: language. The words that are produced seem to be the voice of the 'I' heard in the ear of the 'you', and this is where the issue of voice comes into play. For a poem is a piece of writing, and the reader of the poem is led to reconstruct the voice of the other speaking, and is therefore already complicit in the act, is automatically sympathetic. The reader already begins to be seduced by the act of reading because this act makes a demand on the reader which the reader cannot refuse and still be a reader. Reading is a sympathetic act not just at the psychological level, but at the structural level of what it means to read at all. Of course, a reader may approach a text simply to gain data, for example by reading a phone book or consulting amazon.com. But the reader of a text which contains an 'I', and of one which bears a person's name, can hardly avoid construing that text as if it were a single utterance, as if it came from a 'person', where by 'person' we mean a single, unitary mind – a certain idea of what a person is, in control of its own utterance and of its 'self'.

The reader of 'Prufrock' becomes aware of a person who wishes to master how others see him, and to present himself, as if in a single moment, in terms of a total, fully realized, complete, final, mastered image. So this person is aware of the dangers of misprision – 'That is not what I meant at all' – fears the opinion of others – 'They will say: "How his hair is growing thin!"' – and dreams of manifesting himself in a single moment – 'as if a magic lantern threw the nerves in patterns on a screen': an impossible dream – 'It is impossible to say just what I mean!'.

As outlined in chapter 10, Jacques Derrida has highlighted the widespread existence of the questionable assumption that language can present truth as if in an instant of time and space – as if truth lay beyond time and space. Derrida argues that the real nature of language is to be disseminated in time and space, time being the medium of voice, space that of writing. So there can never be a final moment in which meaning is gathered together as if in a timeless and spaceless moment of prelinguistic truth. 'Prufrock' manifests a nostalgia for the older view of language and a recognition that absolute truths cannot be presented in an instant of time. The universe cannot be rolled up into a ball, presented and summarized, and neither can the self and its voice.

It is not only truth which cannot be so presented; it is the person too, who in his or her very nature is also dispersed throughout time. Ezra Pound's view of 'Prufrock' as a satire seems most notably incorrect at this point. If Prufrock has a tragedy, and if he suffers, what he suffers from is the same immersion within time, the same immersion in a fallen language, and the same being given over to the language of others as anyone else. In this respect, the universality of Prufrock binds the reader to this character quite apart from the particularity of his own circumstance – the frustrated, prudish, ageing Boston dandy.

The poem includes several models of final, emblematic self-presentation of the kind which Prufrock cannot achieve. The epigraph from Dante's *Inferno* presents a person in hell emblematically and forever identified with his crime. The crime motif is reinforced by indirect references in the poem to Dostoevsky's *Crime and Punishment*. That novel deals with murder as a gratuitous act, a murder by a student, Raskolnikov, who believes that it is the ultimate act of self-definition which can put a person above all social rules. The line 'Time to turn back and descend the stair' echoes Raskolnikov's hesitation on the way to the murder, up a flight of stairs. The line 'There will be time to murder and create' echoes Raskolnikov's belief that the gratuitous murder will constitute a self-defining act. Even here, we are aware that the self-defining act cannot really occupy a single moment – Raskolnikov is feverish and in a sense absent from the moment of the murder – but, more than this, the murder only becomes what it is, ritually confirmed within language, by its presentation within language, especially by the confession which follows.

The emphasis on confession (we have already said that the initial line adopts a tone of complicity which we can now see as confessional) is borne out by the references to prophecy – 'I am no great prophet' – where the prophet would be the one whose language can master time, see the future. The reference to John the Baptist, himself emblematically figured in death by his head on a plate, indicates the theological dimension of the issue of presentation: it is God alone who is thought to stand outside time and space, but even God must appear by coming to earth, be anticipated and remembered. Indeed a structure of anticipation and memory is important for the poem, which begins with Prufrock's anticipation, his imaginary attempts to master the instant of his own self-presentation, and concludes with retrospect ('And would it have been worth it, after all'). The moment itself is unmasterable – indeed it did not take place – and while a Hamlet or Raskolnikov appeared to transcend time in decisive action, emblematized forever by the scale of what they had done, Prufrock can achieve no such moment as murder or seducer, in the act of love or even in death.

CHAPTER 3

'The Waste Land', Nancy Cunard and Mina Loy

If 'Prufrock' presents a character who has become merely voice and seeks nostalgically for a moment of triumphal self-presentation, 'The Waste Land' presents a series of voices in which the reader struggles to locate a poetic 'I' in among the various characters who inhabit the text. The initially astonishing, almost collage-like form of 'The Waste Land' came as a surprise perhaps even to the author of the poem, who had consigned a series of manuscripts to his friend Ezra Pound to make editorial suggestions. Pound, who had been working on his *Cantos* for a number of years, had, from Imagist roots, already developed a mode of presentation in which juxtapositions, radical and unexplained shifts of frame of reference and voice, had become the norm. When Pound received Eliot's manuscripts, he set to work excising what he felt to be weaker passages and words, and editing the whole into the continuous sequence which we now know. Some of Pound's changes were dramatic, as in the fourth section, 'Death by Water', where he reduced a lengthy narrative to its final few lines. Eliot queried whether the few remaining lines which Pound was prepared to endorse should go in, since without the original narrative there was nothing to sustain or explain them. Pound, who did not worry about explaining, and who enjoyed the sonorous quiddity of words concisely ordered and laconically 'present' to the reader, had no doubt that these lines *should* remain and pointed out that the reference in the Tarot reading sequence, 'Fear death by water', called for their inclusion.

The result was the first major poem in English that must properly be considered a collaborative effort, and one of the more enigmatic and decentred texts which literature in English had produced up until that time. The apparent 'difficulty' of 'The Waste Land' did not result in a history of rejection or slow uptake. Almost paradoxically, the poem was well received from the moment of its publication in 1922. If it has any problem at all it is not one of underexposure, but of enormous overexposure. For it makes no difference that few are quite sure how this poem is to be interpreted or accounted for; it is as familiar to the modern reader as Gray's (now unfamiliar) 'Elegy' was to an earlier generation. In the day of the French *nouveau roman* or 'new novel' of Robbe-Grillet and others, there was a celebration of a kind of recalcitrant modernism which was said to be '*illisible*' – 'unreadable'. What was meant by this was that the text resisted standard modes of reading and interpretation, in a manner which these neo-modernists regarded as entirely positive. I suggest that 'The Waste Land' also is an *illisible* text, but in an entirely different sense. This text, so recalcitrant perhaps in that moment in which an essay or lecture is called for, suffers in reality from the reverse of *illisibilité*: it is unreadable because it is over-familiar.

There can be no text so illustrative of the effects that the process of familiarization has had on the reception of modernism. From the very outset the poem has been seized upon both as an expression of the modern malaise and as one of the principal sites of modernism itself, and of the modern in literature and art under all of its aspects. For all its apparent modernity, 'The Waste Land' now seems to be one of the least *shocking* of modernist texts, and has settled down perhaps to being merely *irritating*. For early readers the poem reflected discontent and uncertainty after World War I, though how many of those readers located *castration* – actually the poem's governing trope – as the central metaphor for male unease after the war is a moot point. Ernest Hemingway's Jake Barnes in *Fiesta* is generally given the credit for this, with the nearly impotent Leopold Bloom of *Ulysses* a close second. In a very concrete sense, Eliot used the poem to anchor his own career, not merely as a poet but as an editor and cultural commentator, by publishing the poem as the first item in his new journal the *Criterion*, which was used to launch a classicist cultural programme alongside a monarchist political programme that had extensive influence in the interwar decades. Yet Eliot's poem by no means anticipates the programme which it was used to underpin, and when F. R. Leavis, who cited the text as a cornerstone of contemporary literary study, attempts to read it as an extension of Eliot's later cultural pessimism (and as a buttress for Leavis's own pessimism) the effects are strained:

> What is the significance of the modern Waste Land? The answer may be read in what appears as the rich disorganisation of the poem. The seeming disjointedness is intimately related to the erudition that has annoyed so many readers and to the wealth of literary borrowings and allusions. These characteristics reflect the present state of civilization. The traditions and cultures have mingled, and the historical imagination makes the past contemporary; no one tradition can digest so great a variety of materials, and the result is a break-down of forms and the irrevocable loss of that sense of absoluteness which seems necessary to a robust culture. [. . .]
>
> In considering our present plight we have also to take account of the incessant rapid change that characterises the Machine Age. The result is breach of continuity and uprooting of life. This last metaphor has a peculiar aptness, for what we are now witnessing today is the final uprooting of the immemorial way of life, of life rooted in the soil.[1]

I quote this at length because, while it seems loosely to reflect what might almost seem to be a consensual view about the 'disorganiza-tion' of modernity, it is also a cornerstone in a series of attempts to compel the poem to underwrite a broader set of critical and cultural claims. Rather than deal with this passage in too much detail, I will say simply that the generalizations about the 'machine age' and the end of a way of life rooted in the soil do not properly reflect the poem's agenda, and do not explain references to the land in the poem's opening passage, or to the modernity of suburban living in the passage where the clerk meets the typist and she 'smooths her hair with automatic hand, / And puts a record on the gramophone' – although at first glance it might seem to.

We might agree with Leavis that the 'disorganization' of the poem reflects something about the modern mind: the fact that there is now more information, there are more languages and cultures and knowledges, than can be readily assimilated. Even if we are tempted by this account, we might reflect that the other languages and cultures, plus a good deal of technical and scientific knowledge, did exist in earlier centuries, and that the way of dealing with the multifariousness of knowledge had never previously been to pile it all together into one aesthetic object. We might at least think that something about modernity promotes disorganization and confusion of mind; but the few years leading up to the 'The Waste Land' had confirmed in the opinion of many commentators that society had become increasingly centrally controlled and organized, with government and business leading the way in the rapid revolutionary transformation and centralization of society.

The general cultural claims about 'The Waste Land' in its first decades were replaced by a process of scholarly interpretation, which was then followed by a deconstructive phase in which it was possible to argue that the poem really could not be interpreted and in effect meant practically nothing at all: it was a text without an author, the site of readerly speculative play but not of any complex, hidden or buried meaning.

So in relation to this poem we have been asked to note its cultural centrality as an emblem of modernity, to seek 'interpretations' of its only occasionally abstruse 'references' and then, having passed through these processes, to note also that it is a decentred text which seduces a reader with promises of a meaning which, alas, is not to be found.

I have already suggested in the discussion of 'Prufrock' that the notion of voice and a particular model of being trapped in time are at work in Eliot's oeuvre. It would be tempting to insist on an ever deeper radicalization of 'voice' in 'The Waste Land', as the guiding figure of a central character and therefore of a central poetic voice is eclipsed. Eliot's original title was, revealingly, 'He do the police in different voices.'[2] Yet here there is more at work than a simple concatenation of character voices, and also something other at play than the use of literary and other allusions to bolster the central meaning of the poem.

What might it mean, for example, to quote directly four lines of text from Wagner's *Tristan und Isolde*, as Eliot does at lines 31–4?

> Frisch weht der Wind
> Der Heimat zu
> Mein Irisch Kind,
> Wo weilest du?

[The wind is blowing freshly to the homeland. My Irish child, where are you tarrying?]

Here, it is not a matter of catching some erudite allusion which, if we lacked the learning, might escape us all together and impoverish our experience of the poem. We cannot miss this, since it is in German, and since it is taken directly from what in Eliot's own time was already understood to be the single most significant work of modern music and one of the handful of great masterpieces of the operatic stage. There is no missing it then, but if this is an 'allusion', to what does it allude? For the lines quoted are among the first sung in the opera, by a young sailor who is not central to the main action. Moreover they are set to memorable and magnificent music, which once it is discovered must be recalled when these words are encountered in Eliot's text. Without dwelling on the meaning and purpose of the young sailor's words, I would like to move straight to the point that Eliot's purpose in quoting from *Tristan und Isolde* must be in reference to that work's focus on erotic love. We know this, since it is completely clear that erotic love is the focus of Eliot's poem as a whole. The issue for a reader is not to account for the *allusion* (which I have just done), but to account for the poetic method by which not only is a highly relevant, resonant phrase borrowed from another work, but that entire work is imported in synecdoche, any reference to it being sufficient to imply all of the meaning which that work contains.

In terms of its rhetorical form, 'The Waste Land' is both ironic and lyrically confessional. In each of the successive voices which the poem offers, to the extent that we can distinguish between one 'speaker' and another, we are led to ask whether what we hear is the author's own voice, the voice of a character which he stands outside completely, or something in between. Whatever we decide, we acknowledge that the author is not someone directly present in the poem, but an implied entity outside the poem though suggested by it, combining surface elements in a test or game in which we eerily feel something about human suffering in general is reflected. The ironic authorial stance creates promising opportunities for the close readers of poetry and deconstructionists, but by way of providing a more global and less detailed account of the poem than results from such strategies of intensive reading, I offer the following potted thematic summary.

However complicated its rhetorical mode, the meaning of 'The Waste Land' is, I think, comparatively clear. Human beings are confined to an existence given over to reproduction and death. It is a torment to be caught in such a cycle, since our sexuality is something which possesses us and causes us to live unhappy and distorted lives. This is so whether one is a queen or a prostitute. The great religions all deal with the topic of liberation from sex; that is, from the body and from sin. In the case of Christianity, the anthropological studies of James Frazier and Jessie Weston (referred to in Eliot's 'Notes on the Waste Land') tend to reveal that the notion of resurrection, which in Christianity stands for escape from the present way of living, is derived from ancient fertility rituals in which a human sacrifice (of one who has been made king or god for a year) is made to satisfy the gods and ensure a good harvest. This sacrifice has been reinterpreted in Christianity as the resurrection, but it seems that the original pre-Christian narrative, rather than confirming the idea of an escape from the body, confirms instead that we are trapped on earth. The cycle of the seasons continues and the sacrifice is made only to guarantee fertility. So the meaning of the fertility rite which underpins the story of Christ's sacrifice is that we are confined to the cycle of reproduction, not that we can escape it.

The manner in which the Christian story has been mapped on to myths which are themselves the residual record of ancient fertility rituals is made clear in, for example, Thomas Malory's *Morte d'Arthur*. In this fifteenth-century tale of Arthur and his knights, it is apparent that a succession of Christian authors have bestowed Christian meanings on the tales which they retell, tales which in origin reflect pre-Christian narratives themselves based on the notion of ritual sacrifice. It is Malory's text which gives 'The Waste Land' its title. The reference is to a more obscure corner of Malory's narrative in which we learn of a wounded king whose land, like Arthur's, is laid waste because of a mysterious wound which he has received. However, the actions which the hero must take to heal the wound conclude not with the salvation but with the death of the old king (like the annual sacrificial victim), and with the hero subsequently taking his place (thereby fulfilling a cycle: the next year *he* will have become the old king and it will be *his* turn to be sacrificed). This version of the Parsifal story is presented in a more recognizable form by Wagner in his opera, which he called 'An Easter Ritual' in order to emphasize the pagan origin of the Christian tale. The mysterious wound is castration, infertility. It is made by a lance, a symbol of the penis and already in place in the Christian story as the weapon which was used to pierce the side of Christ on the cross. The grail was used to catch the blood which spilt from the wound, and in the story of Arthur it is a sinless man, Parsifal, who must find the grail and restore Arthur's kingdom. The quest for the grail, then, is given a Christian meaning, as if it were concerned with *redemption* from the earth: but the story of the hero's quest to *save* the king and his infertile (waste) land is actually a version of the pre-Christian tale in which the hero is merely the next king-for-a-year, the next sacrificial victim to be pampered for a year and then given over to please the gods and ensure a fertile harvest. In summary, 'The Waste Land' is a lament that, while religion offers the hope of redemption from sin, sex, the body, from the cycle of birth and death, it seems likely that, as the apparent origin of the Christian story in fertility rites seems to suggest, we are confined to a permanent suffering. As a convenient adjunct to this account, it can be argued that the castration element has a heavily concealed biographical aspect for Eliot, in that it seems to reflect an impotence anxiety associated with his wife's reported nymphomania.

Well, I hope readers who consider that important matters have been lost in transit will forgive such a blunt attempt at demystification. Rather than offer an exhaustive account of 'The Waste Land', I would like to give a little attention to some alternative currents in modernist poetry which the example of Eliot has, until recently, all but eclipsed. My summary of 'The Waste Land' did not attract attention to the manner in which the poem is gendered, a complicated issue in the light of the ironic removal of the author and the difficulty of making final, groundable claims about the exact purpose of any particular piece of material which the poem incorporates. Many readers will suspect, unsurprisingly, that this is a sexist poem which has secured its priority through a continued male dominance of the literary canon.

There are alternatives and complements to Eliot in the work of female modernist poets which have only recently begun to come into view. The wealthy socialite Nancy Cunard is celebrated in literature as a changeable and beautiful woman addicted to sex, in Michael Arlen's novel *The Green Hat* (1924) and in Aldous Huxley's *Point Counter Point*

(1928). Cunard can also possibly be identified with Fresca, a character in a portion of the original manuscript of 'The Waste Land', a piece of unsubtle satire in the manner of Pope and with the venom of Swift which Pound understandably rejected.

Cunard was herself a poet, and although she did not pursue the profession with great consistency, her comparatively small output is of intense interest. Most interesting is her long poem *Parallax*, which turns out to be a sustained look at Eliot and a genuinely novel literary form.

Parallax was published by Leonard and Virginia Woolf's Hogarth Press in 1925, three years after 'The Waste Land', and it may have been Virginia Woolf who suggested to Cunard the title for the poem. Woolf in turn may have been aware of its occurrence in *Ulysses*, where the word has a prominent role. It is used by Bloom, who wonders what it means, in the 'Lestrygonians' episode of *Ulysses*.[3] We can of course look directly at the dictionary definition of parallax, and find that it is a term, used particularly in astronomy, to indicate an apparent change in the position of an object due to a change in the position of the observer. The epigraph to Cunard's text is a quotation from Sir Thomas Browne which gives a particular inflection to this general definition: 'Many things are known as some are seen, that is by Paralaxis, or at some distance from their true and proper being.' Helpful as it is in indicating the perspectival relationship of observer and observed as the nub of the title, even the context of the word in the quotation from Browne does not prepare a reader for the unusual form of poetic rhetoric which Cunard presents in this work.

There are large segments of *Parallax* which allude to some of the best-known elements of Eliot's work, in particular to 'The Waste Land', 'The Love Song of J. Alfred Prufrock' and 'Preludes'. The work presents a kind of narrative of an unnamed male protagonist. The first time reader is presented with two curious questions. First, what is the purpose of the extensive allusions to Eliot's work? Second, has Cunard used a male protagonist as an autobiographical mask, or does she intend to present some other actual or fictional protagonist by way of comment on a certain individual or type? These two questions are closely interwoven. The allusions to Eliot's work might appear to be borrowings that reflect the over-dependence of a comparatively novice poet on a series of recent masterpieces which she cannot get out of her mind. However, the sheer extent of the allusions and half quotations seems to belie this, not least because an important section in the centre of the poem (beginning 'Well, instead') appears systematically to exclude all reference to Eliot.

I suggest that Cunard has created a new rhetorical form, over which she has suspended the name 'parallax', in which a systematic reworking and re-presentation of the existing material of a contemporary is used to create a new work. The purpose of this work is to create a kind of third person who is the product of Cunard's reading of Eliot in terms of herself. This hybrid third person is gendered as male to distance him from Cunard, yet elements of her own character (her fondness for wine, something Eliot never signals) and of her own history (her travels) are combined with the reworked and reimagined material from Eliot in such a way that this melancholy bohemian is present as a reading of both Eliot and Cunard, a possible being – but is this a being to be sympathized with or rejected?

The form of the poem creates a continuing ambivalence about this figure, an artist who seeks beauty but is unsure what beauty is, and whose meditations are fuelled and flawed by alcohol. Satire or sympathetic portrait? As revealed by the opening lines, this might be either, the figure described having something in common with the Promethean Byron revealed in book III of *Child Harold's Pilgrimage*:

> He would have every milestone back of him,
> The seas explored, clouds winds and tears encompassed,
> All separate moods unwrapped, made clear.[4]

This over-reacher would seem at first sight to 'be' neither Eliot nor Cunard. How much of Eliot's own search for faith, and how much of his 'Preludes', should we find in the following lines?

> His credo threads
> Doubt with belief, questions the ultimate grace
> That shall explain, atoning.
> A candle drips beside the nocturnal score –
> Dawns move along the city's line reflecting,
> Stare through his rented casement.
>
> (p. 4)

The manner in which Eliot haunts this melancholy figure is hard to pin down. The 'Waste Land' is a tangible presence at certain points:

'On discreet waters / In Battersea I drifted, acquiescent'(p. 10). However, the trajectory of the poem is concerned with the escape from
London, and an attempt to discover alternatives rather than dwell in
its melancholy: 'Well instead – / The south, and its enormous days'
(p. 11). The questions which the voice of the poem poses, and the
manner in which they are posed, appear to be at odds with anything
found in Eliot, questions about obligation to the past and the search
for beauty which are questions about the form and purpose of art:

> Are the living ghosts to the dead, or do the dead disclaim
> This clutch of hands, the tears cast out to them?
> Must one be courteous, halve defunct regrets,
> Present oneself as host to 'Yester-year'?
>
> (p. 11)

The magnificent closing section of the poem ends as an ambiguous
and resonant reworking of elements of 'The Waste Land' which leaves
hanging the status of 'I' and 'you' and all questions concerning the
ownership and location of words. The opening recalls the 'Stetson!' and
'hypocrite lecteur' of 'The Waste Land', the 'I that have walked' is Eliot's
Tiresias, the allusions to Prufrock are clear; but the inflections that these
are given seem both to mirror Eliot and to reflect concerns introduced
by Cunard. The quotation marks are in the original:

> ['. . .] "Hail partner, that went as I
> In towns, in wastes – I, shadow,
> Meet with you – I that have walked with
>   recording eyes
> Through a rich bitter world, and seen
> The heart close with the brain, the brain crossed
>   by the heart –
> I that have made, seeing all,
> Nothing, and nothing kept, nor understood
> Of the empty hands, the hands impotent through
>   Time that lift and fall
> Along a question –
>   Nor of passing and re-passing
> By the twin affirmations of never and for-ever,
>   In doubt, in shame, in silence."'
>
> (p. 24)

I have presented this quotation in such a way as to show both sets of quotation marks within which it appears. It is quite disconcerting to arrive at this potent conclusion only to be reminded that this text is a quoted voice within a quoted voice, a bold rhetorical stroke which goes one step further than Eliot's own use of quotation marks in 'The Waste Land'. Whose voice is it that we hear, at the poem's conclusion? We remain unsure – the effect of parallax, Cunard's particular form of intertextual composition, in which the perspective of both subject and object shifts in the very act of reading. *Parallax*, the masterpiece of Cunard's small oeuvre, still awaits, and invites, more conclusive commentary.

If 'The Waste Land' placed itself at the crux of modernism in poetry, Mina Loy's earlier sequence 'Songs to Joannes' was somehow shifted off the map altogether, and has only in recent years been coming back to wider attention. Loy was presented in her time as an American poet. She was actually English, but more importantly her stays in Paris and Italy had placed her in close contact with prominent avant-gardists, especially the Futurists Giovanni Papini and F. T. Marinetti. No less focused on sex than the widely celebrated 'Waste Land', Loy's 'Songs to Joannes' were published in Alfred Kreymbourg's poetry journal *Others* between 1915 and 1917, not to celebration but to moral outcry. Objections to Loy's scandalous explicitness seem not merely to have delayed the acceptance of hers as a vital and original voice, but to have excluded her from consideration, despite support for her work from normally influential figures such as Ezra Pound.

It is a pity that Loy's work in general, and 'Songs' in particular, has had to struggle for recognition, not least because she emerges as a significant innovator who absorbed European influences, transformed them into an original idiom, and in turn quietly influenced other poets whose voices reached beyond hers. The most direct example of such influence is perhaps Loy's 'At the Door of the House', which features an account of a Tarot reading that is not so much echoed in as transposed into 'The Waste Land':

> This   is the Devil
> And these two skeletons
> Are mortifications
> You   are going to make a journey.[5]

The use of spaces within lines is characteristic of Loy, and is an innovation that requires a new kind of pause, and which seems to insist on the character of a word or phrase before it is absorbed into the shape and cadence of the sentence. Loy may have been adapting ideas from Marinetti's 1913 'Manifesto', which called for the 'destruction of syntax' and argued for the use of a free, expressive orthography which would restore the freshness of the original lyrical impulse of poetry – 'words in freedom'.[6] Loy certainly did not mimic the complete orthographic liberty of works such as Marinetti's *Zang, Tumb Tuum* (1914), nor is 'Songs' a response to the 1913 *Futurist Manifesto of Lust*, which crudely equated art and war as 'manifestations of sensuality.'[7] Instead, 'Songs' follows on in part from her own 1914 *Feminist Manifesto*, which argued that 'sex or so-called love must be reduced to its initial element, honour, grief, sentimentality, pride & consequently jealousy must be detached from it'.[8]

In 'Songs to Joannes', Loy produces a dry, free mode of speech, at times elliptic, which tells the non-continuous story of (a) relationship in 34 short lyric episodes. She uses this free and comparatively open form to express certain moments of possible relationship between a man and woman in terms of both love and sex, examining, always with care, the nature and purpose of the difference between the two protagonists. The occasionally disjointed syntax, the careful use of free verse (including spacing) to veil and unveil potential meanings, and the slippage among possible points of view make 'Songs' a rich model of alternatives to the conventions of the sonnet sequence.

The stunning opening, though it does not set the tone for what is, after all, a varied sequence, is often quoted:

> Spawn   of   Fantasies
> Silting the appraisable
> Pig Cupid   his rosy snout
> Rooting erotic garbage
> 'Once upon a time'
> Pulls a weed   white star-topped
> Among wild oats   sown in mucous membrane.
>
> (p. 53)

The disguised genital imagery may be what first strikes the reader, though this passage would be curiously hard to censor because it is hard to construe. The line breaks and spacing, the use of quotation marks, disguise that this is probably a single sentence following a non-existent colon after 'Fantasies' – main verb, 'pulls' – and with a parenthesis around 'Once upon a time'. Only the 'mucous membrane' seems literal, the rest a mixture of metaphors that only hint at the genital references which are their inevitable though somehow unrecuperable origin.

Though early readers were shocked – and there is no doubt that shock was part of the whole Futurist ethos which Loy absorbed – it is hard to stay shocked when it becomes evident that Loy is trying to examine the nature of bohemian love precisely in terms of its lack of commitment, its sensuousness, the fragility of the relationships that unmarried love can offer, and the simple uncertainty of trying to pursue love *as* love in a context in which the regular consequence of heterosexual love – marriage – is being disavowed. Disavowed by whom? Not simply by that element in Loy which had produced the *Feminist Manifesto*, not simply by artists and writers who consider themselves 'geniuses' whose individuality is sacrosanct, but also by a collective change of social environment among the young and independent which is found certainly in the England of this period and which evidently Loy found too in the Paris and Florence of the 1910s.

The work of D. H. Lawrence can be reckoned among the most consistent in its documentation of the bohemian approach to free love, although it is very evident that *Lady Chatterley's Lover* is the culmination of a campaign against free love, which uses its close examination of the bodily and verbal nature of sex and sexuality to press for an entirely different kind of authenticity from that which Loy's verse seeks. However, 'Songs' is closely akin to *Lady Chatterley's Lover*, and to other of Lawrence's works, in its attempt to body forth nuances of sexual relationship that remained, from a literary point of view at least, hitherto obscure.

Section XVI begins 'We might have lived together / In the lights of the Arno', and goes on to list other things 'we' might have done before concluding: 'And never known any better' (p. 59). This means both that 'better' might be impossible, and that by having stayed together neither might have had the chance to 'know better' (that is, with another). However we read it, the conditional 'might' reveals already that the affair is a thing of the past, and this is a lament for how things might have been. Should this lost future be lamented? In section XIII, one voice advocates that one must remain separate from the other to protect the genius of individual vision – 'Or we might make an end of the jostling of aspirations / Disorb inviolate egos' – while another voice – ironically? – notes the risk that 'we might tumble together / Depersonalized / Identical / Into the terrific Nirvana / Me you – you – me' (p. 58).

The entire sequence plays off the differing lures of the 'inviolate ego' and the 'terrific Nirvana'. At this time there was revived interest in the 'egoism' of Max Stirner, whose *The Ego and his Own* (1844) had so aroused the indignation of his fellow Hegelians, Karl Marx and Friedrich Engels, for its (to them) one-sided assertion of the particularity of selfhood over socially determined moral rules. Stirner's book was published in English translation in 1912 and seems to have acquired a new audience. Notably, Dora Marsden, who like other cultural intellectuals of the period was looking for an alternative to suffragism, relaunched her journal the *New Freewoman* as the *Egoist* in 1914, not only in tribute to Stirner, but as a reflection of a departure from the moralizing norms of the suffrage movement (which as a by-line advocated sexual abstinence). Wyndham Lewis, himself influenced by Stirner, wrote in a *Blast* (1914): 'BEYOND ACTION AND REACTION WE WILL ESTABLISH OURSELVES', echoing Stirner; but, in the desire to signal that he had gone beyond even this latest novelty has his character Argol throw Stirner's book out of the window in his play *Enemy of the Stars* (also published in *Blast*, 1914). The relationship between sexual love and art was the topic of Lewis's novel, *Tarr* (1918) (see below, chapter 5).

'Songs to Joannes' reflect on the troubled world that a feminist must inhabit who has renounced existing feminism in favour, however ambivalent, of a cult of ego and genius. The passing references to the ego serve to illuminate this context for Loy's poetic musings by showing the context of this word (which has nothing to with the Freudian ego as it is used here). We sometimes find writers of Loy's generation calling for 'honesty' in expression. Pound used the word frequently. They did so because they felt that the truth of individual existence was masked by bourgeois convention. In particular, the truths about individual desires were smothered by the bourgeois convention of marriage. In searching for new modes of writing, writers were also keen to access, embody and even bring about new truths.

Not all remained optimistic and, as we have seen, 'The Waste Land' tends to identify modernism as a somewhat pessimistic and recondite or even elitist movement. Loy offers something different. She writes about love in an idiom which is forged to mirror, in however fragmented a fashion, truths and aspects of a mode of being that were not readily available in art. It is not clear that this new mode of being, which takes shape in the changing attitudes and practices of bohemians and artists, will yield happiness or anything resembling a 'love' which is now more elusive than ever. Yet love will continue to supply a motive for art, as section XXXIV signals with its single laconic line:

> Love – – – the preeminent litterateur.
>
> (p. 68)

CHAPTER 4

Wallace Stevens and Romantic Legacy

Imagism sought its rationale in objectivity. Eliot's words were aware of their curious status as objects which belonged to subjects, and his poetry constantly foregrounds their mysterious modality. Stevens's work resists the apparent objectivity of Imagism. Unlike Eliot, he is not concerned to foreground the instability of language and subject as they stand in relation to each other. Instead, the work of Wallace Stevens, beginning with *Harmonium* (1923) and *Ideas of Order* (1935), follows the Romantics in asserting the primacy of imagination (see chapter 10). His poetry treats imagination not as passive or receptive, but as the active agency which forms the world. However, this does not mean that the imagination is like a post-Impressionist painter, treating representation of the world as something to be shifted around to satisfy the artist's sense of form. Rather, imagination takes place in the form of words themselves, above all in the syntax of words as they unfold in an endless process of making a world. In particular, Stevens's work constantly utilizes the poles of subject and object as facts of language, and toys playfully with all the paradoxes which this seemingly inescapable binary opposition creates.

Stevens's poetry displays a highly self-conscious awareness of its relationship to the romantic legacy. Ezra Pound and William Carlos Williams had tried to restore 'things' to verse, in one manner or another, willing words to be almost thing-like and seeming nearly to reject subject or mind, as in Williams's famous phrase: 'no ideas but in things'.[1] Stevens's verse remains convinced that the abolition of rhetoric, the transparent self-presence of words, and the Romantic restoration of nature, remain impossible goals. For Stevens, the non-identity of mind and world is built into the structure of mind and world, and into the structure of language itself, and we would do better to take account of the complex consequences that arise from this than to seek to abolish the difference by claiming an absolute 'objectivity' of words or, indeed, of things.

The duality of subject and object, of mind and nature, of the thinking and the non-thinking, remains firmly embedded within the mind, and within the whole project of Stevens's poetry, where the mind and its object are in constant motion and constant play – something he indicates with one of his titles: 'The Pleasures of Merely Circulating'.

In writing 'In a Station of the Metro', Pound claimed that he had attempted to capture 'the precise instant when a thing outward and objective transforms itself, or darts into a thing inward and subjective'.[2] Pound's conception is almost scientific: the poem is to be a 'record'. Moreover, Pound's model supposes a separation of language and experiential or aesthetic event, so there is a prelinguistic event or experience which the subject undergoes, and this can be later documented in language. The language serves the purpose of restoring to the reader some sense of the original prelinguistic experience, so language itself is a just a carrier, something to be overcome or seen through. As we have seen in our discussion of Pound, this leads in his work to a modelling of language as thing-like, as being concerned primarily with a correspondence of word and thing, and to a resistance to what he calls 'rhetoric' (grammar and syntax), which in the 'Metro' poem is almost abolished. Structure is reduced to the juxtaposition, akin to a simile, implied by the colon or semicolon separating the two segments of the poem.

Stevens and Pound actually start from the same point, but their destinations are very different. The common starting point concerns the notion of aesthetic experience and the possibility of its embodiment in art, in language. The separation occurs at the very instant of departure. Unlike Pound, Stevens does not see the aesthetic experience as occupying an instant of time, but as something deployed through time. He does not see it as something that lies outside language, something prelinguistic, but as something which is embedded in understanding and therefore in language. He does not see it as something that affects only the senses, but as something which belongs to mind. Especially, he does not see the experience as something tied to one sense, but as something which moves through the senses. Finally, he does not regard an aesthetic experience as complete, ended, summarized, confined within time, or space, or within any part of the mind, but as something open, incomplete, challenging our ability to shape, recall, represent, challenging even mind's ability actually and fully to undergo it.

Unlike Pound, Stevens sees poetry as basically discursive. He does not, however, think of writing as something that can transcend and fix experience, but as immanent to experience, permanently circulating within it, indeed *constituting* it. So language, though it is a discourse, is not a discourse of finality, but of openness. Statements often remain structurally incomplete or ambivalent; negatives are numerous, almost predominant, as if to say what something is not, to state what it cannot be equated with, creates as much movement of understanding as any positive statement. Stevens asserts the incompleteness of experience against the affirmation of experience as a totality.

In this respect, Stevens's work demonstrates a rich intercourse with the poetry of the British Romantics, as well as with the sequence of ideas which flowed from Immanuel Kant and the flowering of German Romanticism in reaction to Kant. I would like here to emphasize the poetic connection, in order to mitigate the impression which might otherwise be created that Stevens is basically a philosophical poet. He is not; Stevens is basically an aesthete, where that term has a very strict post-Christian connotation. While William Wordsworth and Samuel Taylor Coleridge (if not John Keats) basically looked on nature as something which in one manner or another stemmed from God, Stevens's universe is a disenchanted one, as his poem 'A High-Toned Old Christian Woman' shows. While Coleridge and Wordsworth always entertain the idea that engagement with nature through the senses has a theological dimension, this is unavailable to Stevens. In any case, the tradition of puritanical Christianity with which this Bostonian is engaged varies considerably from the models entertained by Wordsworth and Coleridge. The substantial difference is this, however: it is one matter if the experience of the senses is referred ultimately to an entity (God) which lies outside the senses, another matter altogether if sense experience is merely an end in itself. If there is no God, then sense experience is not something that can restore a soul and make it at home in the world, but is a pleasure which by its very definition is always slipping away.

Experience is underpinned not by God but by death. Stevens movingly documents this knowledge in his poem 'Waving Adieu, Adieu, Adieu':

> In a world without heaven to follow, the stops
> Would be endings, more poignant than partings, profounder,
> And that would be saying farewell, repeating farewell,
> Just to be there and just to behold.[3]

'They practice, / Enough, for heaven', the text declares, referring to the Christian attitude to the afterlife, as the poem discovers a terrible theology of its own: it is not that the moment brings the subject nearer to God, rather that every passing instant is consigned irretrievably to God. To say 'Adieu', literally consigning 'to God' a person who is about to disappear from your sight, counters religious rites which anticipate a future union with God, by making of mortality itself a ritual of constant surrender to irreversible passage.

This constant passage is the main and most impressive feature of Stevens's work. It is an extrapolation from and reinflection of key features of Romantic poetry. In the 'Preface' to *Lyrical Ballads*, Wordsworth described poetry as originating in 'emotion recollected in tranquillity'. Recollection is important for Wordsworth in two ways. Principally, he refers to the involuntary or voluntary recollection of experiences with nature and their associated moods. However, it is also clear from his work that the reflection on the meaning of experience is an integral part of the process. So with Wordsworth it is not merely that an experience is undergone, but that writing must attempt the recollection of the experience and reflection must act to interpret its significance. This structure is reproduced time and again in his writing, and firmly links experience to memory and reflection. His famous poem 'I wandered lonely as a Cloud' reflects this structure. In its original, three-stanza version, the first two stanzas describe the original moment of seeing the daffodils; the poet is absorbed in the moment, transfixed, but does not consciously grasp the meaning of his experience: 'I gazed – and gazed – but little thought / What wealth the shew to me had brought.'[4] The final stanza of the poem describes the involuntary recollection of this incident, the mood-altering flash of visual memory, in which the sight of the daffodils in effect 'pays off':

> For oft when on my couch I lie
> In vacant or in pensive mood,
> They flash upon that inward eye
> Which is the bliss of solitude.

Wordsworth is quite different from Stevens, however in his almost capitalist optimism that experience is like a large accumulated investment on which he can draw. The ego in Wordsworth is strangely powerful, and the analysing mind can quite separate itself from the aesthetic experiences which it has undergone. So although this model of experience of nature plus reflection on that experience can be found in Wordsworth, it is in Keats that we find an ego more akin to that of Stevens, for in Keats the self does not transcend its moments of experience, but is tormented by the fact that the self, like experience, must die. Wordsworth's analysing ego is a transcendental one; that of Keats is thrown into being and given over to death, unable confidently to master its own situation. For Keats, aesthetic experience torments us with thoughts of death; it does not provide the buffer of relief from the bustle of everyday life which Wordsworth always recommends.

In Keats as in Stevens, the aesthetic is given over to death. Stevens's poem 'Waving Adieu, Adieu, Adieu' recalls Keats's 'Ode to a Nightingale', which repeats the word 'Adieu' three times in its concluding stanza. Like 'Ode on a Grecian Urn', this poem dramatizes an ego given over to death, one which cannot master or wholly absorb its moment of experience of the aesthetic, and one above all which finds in one instance sensory fulfilment, in another a sense of loss and absence.

Stevens only occasionally demonstrates this kind of full-blown Keatsian melancholy, and more often than not finds joy rather than sorrow in the pleasure of being given over to an inconclusive experience. Even though we have differentiated Stevens from Wordsworth in this respect, it is Wordsworth rather than Keats who provides the nearest early example of an important aspect of Stevens's style in the prosody of *The Prelude*. A key feature of this style is its syntax and grammar, particularly its mode of developing long arguments as sentences running across many lines. These arguments are characterized by reservations, negatives and hesitations, features that can be found in those sections of the *Prelude* in which Wordsworth finds himself unable to state in conclusive and summary form what the overarching metaphysical description of the meaning of a certain moment actually might be, as in this example from book XIII:

> it appeared to me
> The perfect image of a mighty Mind,
> Of one that feeds upon infinity,
> That is exalted by an underpresence,
> The sense of God, or whatso'er is dim
> Or vast in its own being.[5]

The equivocation here, around 'God, or whatso'er', is one rendered possible by the characteristically expansive mode of *The Prelude*. Stevens finds many other ways to equivocate in his aesthetic descriptions, and makes the manner of the highly structured deferral of summary meaning his own, but the debt to Wordsworth, as to Keats, is clear.

The early poem 'The Snow Man' is a clear manifesto of Stevens's engagement with the Romantic tradition of negotiating the relationship between mind and nature, as well as a key announcement of a commitment to grammar and syntax as the grounding of poetic activity. As in many of Stevens's poems, the occasion of the utterance would seem to be an event of the kind that might lend itself to an Imagistic treatment – an 'epiphany' in which a man looks at a snow man in the middle of a landscape, and has a flash of insight of some kind – a moment in which 'a thing outward and objective transforms itself, or darts into a thing inward and subjective'. If at first glance this poem looks like a Romantic epiphany, the very process by which it unfolds denies the reader any easy grasp of the 'moment' of the poem, and even the apparent common sense of the distinction between the inner world of the mind and the outer world of nature breaks down under the poem's scrutiny.

The first line of the poem is immediately disorienting, as it announces a strange-seeming claim which will be unfolded over the ensuing lines, the shape of which will only fall into place – and then only uncertainly – once the final line is reached. 'One must have a mind of winter', announces the first line, seeming at first to evoke a common usage of 'having a mind of' as 'paying attention to' or 'taking account of'. This sense never disappears, but is gradually eclipsed by the realization that to 'have a mind of winter' is more literal – one must have a mind 'of winter' just as one might have a dress 'of silk'. But in what sense can a mind be 'of winter', and why the imperative of 'must'? The material of Stevens's poem is the manner in which language seeks to articulate the relationship between mind and nature. Here 'mind' stands clearly for mind, while 'winter' is both nature and in particular the notion that nature or the external world affects mind and may reflect it. The poem takes as its starting point the commonplace literary assumption that the weather can reflect the state of mind of a person or character, and toys with the fact that, while mind and world must inhabit each other, must operate in parallel with each other, are unthinkable without each other, yet mind does not merely mirror nature but is engaged in an unending process of identification and disidentification, of submitting to nature and of positing itself as an alternative to nature, something outside the world and independent of it. Winter, here, is used in one way as an example, to test the common notion that the season of winter might reflect a state of depression in the subject. More than this, Stevens establishes a symbolic vocabulary of his own around the seasons. His symbolism is sometimes discussed as if it were extremely fixed, but even where it appears distinct and definite we would be unwise to regard our glosses on it as exhaustive and final. However, it is, at the very least, broadly useful to think of 'winter' in Stevens as a state in which the impact of nature is diminished and the mind is thrown back on the resources of imagination, while 'summer' reflects the antithesis of this position, the domination of the real and the diminished power of imagination in the face of the riot of actuality which the abundance of summer produces.

The rhetorical motion of this poem serves to create uncertainty, as the reader's mind attempts to map what appears to be a complex or elusive proposition, ending in a seeming paradox. The statement that the poem articulates is that 'one must have a mind of winter' to believe that nature does not reflect human feelings. The phrase 'pathetic fallacy' has been used since Ruskin to refer to the literary device which attributes human characteristics to parts of nature; the phrase suggests that it is a 'fallacy' to believe that nature reflects human concerns and moods in this way. Stevens's text suggests that only a 'mind of winter' could believe this to be a fallacy, only a 'mind of winter' could see and hear the effects of winter in the ice and the wind and *not* think 'Of any misery in the sound of the wind'. The argument of the poem throws attention back constantly on the 'mind of winter' in the first line, and the concluding lines suggest a mysterious logic which heightens the intellectual tension. The poem closes with a 'listener' who, 'nothing himself, beholds / Nothing that is not there and the nothing that is'.

We should not here insist on any one exhaustive reading of these final lines, evidently intended to 'tease us out of thought' as much as Keats's urn. Evidently the focus is on the mind/world relation, and the issue is whether the mind can perceive reality without imaginatively enhancing it. The only mind which can perceive the non-human world, without seeing or hearing anything human in it, is the 'mind of winter', the mind so metaphorically cold that it does not see winter as the analogue of human misery, a mind that may indeed not be the mind of a real 'man' at all but of a 'snow man', an effigy of a human being whose mind is indeed 'of' winter because he has a head of snow, part of the very essence of winter, and not a mind perceiving it at all.

The aim of Stevens's texts is not to articulate any full and final position, but to toy with the grammatical and lexical structures with which both poetry and philosophy have articulated the dualism which is the seemingly insuperable legacy of Descartes. Stevens's work circulates possible structures of ideas in a manner which is playful but also intently serious in its implicit critique of – I really want to say, its constant 'worrying' away at – models of the mind/world relation which are inadequate in thought and reductively final.

The poetry will frequently make the point that the whole notion of a mind regarding nature in solitude – the notion on which so much of Wordsworth's work rests – is an insufficient fiction which disregards the necessity that the regarded world must contain other creatures, other humans, and artefacts which are produced by humans. So the mind which thinks it can experience itself in relation to an unminded nature is already engaged in a reductive insistence, even though the basic fact that the non-human is forever within the gaze (and therefore within the mind) is undeniably the case. So the nature that one beholds already reflects back a human as well as a non-human presence, not least because the imagination brings to it an enhancement which is unavoidable and which renders mind and nature strictly unthinkable without each other.

'Thirteen Ways of Looking at a Blackbird' presents a challenge to the Imagist tradition of H. D. and Ezra Pound. This is a sequence of 13 short pieces, each of which seems to attempt an Imagist grasp on a given subject, that of the blackbird. While Imagism seemed to emphasize the finality of the single presentation it discovered – especially in the case of Pound's 'In a Station of the Metro', which he called a 'report' – Stevens presents different 'views'. He does not do so as a way of getting nearer to the truth, but rather in each explores what he takes to be the flawed assumption, of aestheticism in general and of Imagism in particular, that a moment of experience can be contained and re-presented in the poem. So each of the 13 components of 'Blackbird' is a dry and concise exercise in showing how any experience exceeds the frame of the senses, of the mind, and of the language intended to contain and demarcate it.

Each section of 'Blackbird' gently explodes Imagist theory and Romantic convention. Take the first section:

> Among twenty snowy mountains,
> The only moving thing
> Was the eye of the blackbird.[6]

Stevens's texts teases away at the conceit that an image can be seized by the mind, reflecting that the perspective required to offer a single point of view (of a scene or landscape) is already a compression of the impossibly sublime contrast of perspectives inherent in nature – the vastness of the mountains contrasted with the tiny blackbird's eye. There is more, for the phrase 'only moving' creates a substantial pause typical of Stevens. On the one hand 'moving' has the connotation of 'causing emotion' – the prime requisite of poetry might be that it creates feeling or mood. On the other hand, this is a literal claim that the only thing physically 'moving' is the blackbird's eye (we might expect to hear that the blackbird itself is in motion because in flight). Since the only thing in motion is the eye of the blackbird we might also conclude that there is no human observer here (who would also be in motion), as in 'The Snow Man'. There are many other details in this finely condensed, aphoristic work that can be pursued according to the logic which it is Stevens's delight to create; not least the wonderful touch that the mountains which should supply a sublime because vast and quasi-infinite backdrop (according to Romantic tradition) still in fact number an exact 20 (or an approximate 20?), a fact which the scanning eye would not take in even if the counting mind later made such a reckoning.

If 'Thirteen Ways of Looking at a Blackbird' is a sequence of spanners in the works, each component jamming the wheels of a machine which thought itself well oiled, 'The Idea of Order at Key West' is something more of a position piece which makes explicit a stance towards the Romantic legacy in terms that can be clearly mapped out.

Like several important Romantic poems, 'Key West' is organized around the recollection of a significant, heightened moment of aesthetic experience. The whole poem is a retrospect, but falls into two parts, the first and longer dealing with the experience, the second dealing with the aftermath and the process of reflection on the experience. In outline, the shape of the poem follows the model of 'I wandered Lonely as a Cloud'. However, the procedure is considerably more complex. If Wordsworth had predicated a mind contemplating a non-human nature in solitude, Stevens's poem postulates a joint experience of a 'we' which in the latter part of the poem becomes a 'you' and 'I', suggesting dialogue about the nature of the experience which has been undergone. Moreover, the experience is not merely one of mute nature, though it is an experience of the sea, but also includes another human being, an un-named, unspecified 'she':

> She sang beyond the genius of the sea.
>
> The sea was not a mask. No more was she.
>
> For she was the maker of the song she sang.
>
>   It was her voice that made
> The sky acutest at its vanishing.
> She measured to the hour its solitude.
> She was the single artificer of the world
> In which she sang.[7]

The frame of the experience includes not only the 'she', but her singing – her art, an artefact but not an object. This structure enables Stevens to suggest that there is no frame which can contain the non-human (nature) while excluding the human (art). Thus it is not the non-human which appears to the mind in a moment of heightened solitary awareness, but the non-human and the human (nature and art) which are articulated together, forever imbricated, to a mind which is not solitary but social and can both share experience as a 'we' and reflect on it as an 'I' talking to a 'you'. In the equation of pronouns which provides the poles of this poem, 'we', 'she', 'I' and 'you' are supplemented by 'it' – a quietly crucial word in Stevens.

The term 'it' appears in Stevens with a dual function. One function is to refer to the non-human world. The sea in 'Key West' is the amorphous non-human which is given human shape or voice or connotation by the 'she' who walks and sings by it. The water is 'Like a body wholly body, fluttering its empty sleeves'. This phrase, which follows 'The Snow Man' in suggesting the difficulty of not seeing nature anthropomorphically, highlights the recurrent term 'it' as the pronoun which stands for the non-human in contrast to the 'she', the human 'maker' or poet, whose pronominal existence disturbingly melds into the near identity of 'she/sea'. In this first function of the term 'it', there is a clear reference: that is, the subject can straightfor-wardly refer to the inhuman by the term 'it', as if the name or the language could confidently contain everything that was non-human. However, non-human nature is precisely non-linguistic, and language itself has a material or non-meaningful dimension. It is this materiality of language on which the second function of 'it' has a bearing. For 'it' occurs in Stevens frequently as a particle of speech which, while it is essential to the articulation of meaning, has no reference in itself: 'it was more than that'; 'it would have been'. The recurrence of 'it' in Stevens might at first not call attention to itself, but he plays a subtle game, even seeming to have selected words at key junctures which simply contain the syllable 'it' as, here, in the phrase 'veritable ocean', where the non-referential 'it' sits in the middle of the term 'verity' with its reference to the possibility of truthful transparency – a transparency which the material opacity of the sign tends to deny.

If these pronouns are the poles of 'The Idea of Order at Key West', it is the motion of sentence and clause which is the mainspring of the poem's work. Stevens is surely in the camp of Keats who, in his famous odes, saw aesthetic experience as tantalizing, incomplete, unable to be brought definitively within any single frame. Stevens goes further even than Keats in considering an experience not as an instant, but as an unfolding of instants, where actuality blends into aftermath, and where language searches to encapsulate experience in a succession of definitions which are constantly made to recognize the insufficiency of their grammatical subject–predicate–object form. Two devices which appear here in important roles are the paired succession of phrases and the negative. In the former Stevens adjoins two clauses each intended as a possible means of mapping the phenomenon at hand, but by the juxtaposition causes each phrase to reveal the other as a mere effect of grammar. In the phrase 'its [i.e. the ocean's] mimic motion / Made constant cry, caused constantly a cry', the rephrasing suggests alternative or complementary ways of modelling the manner in which nature expresses itself as art, or the way in which the non-human becomes the human, the 'cry' being the primal cry which is the most fundamental form of human expression. Of course, even the paraphrase which I have offered is clumsy and does not do justice to the inferences, both light and complex, which Stevens's text establishes. Does nature itself 'cry'? No, though the sound it makes might be heard by a human as a cry. Does nature 'cause' a cry in the human observer? Well, it may elicit or provoke a cry, but the notion of 'cause' belongs to the mechanics of cause and effect within nature, not to the relationship between mind and nature, which cannot be thought of as one of mere mechanical causality.

Stevens's use of the negative is another key rhetorical device of these poems. Many statements are phrased as negative claims: 'The sea was not a mask. No more was she.' In such phrases, Stevens reveals that the work of his verse is a playful testing of possible statements about the aesthetic, where the pleasure of the poem's work is in the process of sifting and rejection, but also of temporary, partial affirmation. Here the poem confidently rejects the notion that reality is a mask. This is the thesis of Melville's maniacal Ahab, who declares 'All visible objects, man, are but as pasteboard masks', and concludes 'If man will strike, strike through the mask!'[8] For Ahab, as for the Puritan mind which is a recurrent object of dislike in Stevens, reality is a surface of signs to be penetrated and construed as meaning. Stevens's poem rejects as facile the assumption that the non-human is merely a sign, expression of a quasi-human intention. So the negative here has a definite function, but to shape a positive statement is less easy, since the truth of the matter shifts endlessly before the grammar which cannot finally contain it.

How do nature and mind enter into relation with each other? Stevens's poem rises to seeming affirmation of the primacy of imagination – 'She was the single artificer of the world / In which she sang' – yet any answer which takes the form of language already belongs to mind and cannot finally close the gap with nature. The whole of Stevens's art is found in the lucid play of logic and sonority around this irreducible paradox.

CHAPTER 5

Wyndham Lewis: Genius and Art

Romanticism had celebrated the artist himself or herself as being at the centre of art, as if the art-work were important because of the genius which lay behind it. The emphasis on the artist over the art-work had been consolidated by the Victorian cult of great men, and worried over by poets such as Browning and Tennyson, who frequently return to the topic of artistic ego. Over the course of the nineteenth century we can see a general shift in the evaluation of the figure of the artist or poet. In the early Romantic period the poet's imagination is celebrated as an identification of the sources of creation itself. Samuel Taylor Coleridge's *Biographia Literaria* (1817) defined what he called 'primary imagination' as 'the living power and prime agent of all human perception, and as a repetition in the finite mind of the eternal act of creation in the infinite I AM'.[1] The 'eternal act of creation' is God's act, and on this view the artist, in possessing this kind of imagination as well as what Coleridge calls a 'secondary' or creative imagination, is in a privileged position both to grasp creation and to re-express it, in an almost God-like fashion. In the later nineteenth century there is a shift to a view of the artist as a privileged aesthete, uniquely placed to enjoy the pleasures and riches of the senses, a view developed by Walter Pater in works such as *Marius the Epicurean* (1885), and both celebrated and queried in Oscar Wilde's *The Picture of Dorian Gray* (1891). This later nineteenth-century view reflected an atheism which left the artist unable to identify with creation itself, but still able to celebrate the precious particularity of his or her own senses and mind.

Whether as genius or aesthete, then, the nineteenth century celebrated and privileged the person of the artist, and modernists found themselves constantly dealing with this legacy. This is one of the things which is at stake when figures such as T. S. Eliot and Ezra Pound insist on a revival of 'classicism' in some form to offset the dominance of 'romanticism'. What they mean by this is that they wish to return to a notion of art which focuses on the art object rather than on the perceptions and emotions of the individual artist. Yet both Pound and Eliot are immersed in Romantic ideas, especially in their early work, and neither tries to get away altogether from the idea of the artist, whom Pound sees as an important trans- mitter of social and political ideas, and whom Eliot sees as a figure veiled but not eliminated by the layering of apparently 'impersonal' text.

Romanticism and its Victorian aftermath left modernism a complex inheritance which was challenged by social shifts combined with historical events. Specifically, the development of a mass working class, and the socialist and communist ideas which accompanied that development, along with the massive slaughter of World War I, combined to place pressure on the notion of the artist as an especially privileged figure. In a history which appeared so dominated by the mass movement of people, whether in war or politics, the rights and role of the self-declaredly 'sensitive' individual became doubtful even to those who believed themselves possessed of such sensitivity.

Although we have used the term 'sensitivity' it would be wrong to assume that art before the war had assumed a stance of passive recep- tivity and wealthy refinement. Certainly, the notion of the artist as aesthete was a class-bound one, tending to emphasize the consump- tion of the riches of the senses which came with material wealth. At the same time, art was the expression of those who were not involved in wealth generation and commerce, who tended to see industrialists and their like as uneducated and 'philistine' – a term describing lack of culture promulgated by Matthew Arnold in *Culture and Anarchy* (1869). In some other countries of Europe, in the period before World War I, artists and writers aggressively confronted the bourgeoisie, asserting the autonomy of art as an end in itself, and as the negation of the life of the bourgeoisie, which was considered to be not merely materialist, complacent and philistine, but also repressive of human sensory, erotic and personal possibilities.

These 'avant-gardists' were so called because they considered themselves to represent the few who had to advance into unknown territory in order that the rest of society could follow. Their programmes were sometimes predominantly artistic, sometimes predominantly social. Their existence across Europe accounts in large part for the tendency to speak about modernism in the arts, but in the case of Britain this presents a small paradox. Britain did not evolve an avant-garde of the same kind as those found in France, Germany, Italy and elsewhere in the decade or so preceding World War I – groups such as the Cubists, Expressionists and Futurists. So the avant-garde when it appears in Britain does so through a process of adaptation from and reinterpretation of other European models.

Of the most prominent British modernists, the painter and writer Wyndham Lewis was perhaps the single figure most closely in contact with European practices and the one most singularly confronted with the question of what it meant to inherit, adapt and depart from the procedures of the European avant-garde. The idea of the artist in Lewis's complex oeuvre is conditioned by three currents; first, the domestic current of Paterian and Wildean aestheticism; second, the Futurism of the Italian F. T. Marinetti; third, the assertion of the superior will found in the work of three nineteenth-century German thinkers, Max Stirner's *The Ego and his Own* (1844), Arthur Schopenhauer's *The World as Will and Idea* (1819) and Friedrich Nietzsche's *Thus Spake Zarathustra* (1883–5).

What Lewis took from each of these influences was the notion that the superior mind of the artist or thinker was a quality which set him apart from society. I say 'him' because these sources routinely set the male against the female, confining the female to unreflecting society while the male strove to overcome the merely social. Lewis was aware of this gendering of the idea of will or genius and used his novel *Tarr* to make the case for female 'genius'. However, while many Romantic and later nineteenth-century thinkers had seen the artist in an optimistic light, perhaps as the harbinger of future social revolution, Lewis was pessimistic about the meaning of the artist's separation from society. He came to see himself as 'The Enemy', an alienated figure who opposed the development of modern capitalist mass society. Moreover, Lewis came to see modernism in the arts in general not as an antithesis to capitalist society, but as the extension of it. He believed that the celebration of time found in the work of his contemporaries and friends, such as James Joyce and Pound, was not opposed to the times but very much in line with them – capitalism too celebrated time and incessant change, with the intention of asserting itself and destabilizing the individual.

The evolution of Lewis's views is one of the most complex and interesting literary and artistic phenomena of modernism, though it is little known because his works are numerous and demanding. In his early work, we find a member of the avant-garde who seeks to imitate the Cubists in his painting and the Italian Futurists in his writing. The early Lewis is found most famously in the journal *Blast*, which he published in two numbers in 1914 and 1915. The optimistic avant-gardist is still present in his novel *Tarr* (1918, revised 1928). After World War I, he retreats into a state of pessimism about the development of mass society which is similar to the pessimism found in the work of Eliot and D. H. Lawrence. This pessimism is expressed in polemical works including *The Art of Being Ruled* (1926), a denunciation of mass society, and *Time and Western Man* (1927), a critique of modernist writing and modern philosophy. There are also important creative works, including *The Childermass* (1928), an amazing if neglected philosophical fantasy, and *The Apes of God* (1930), a densely written satire on the corrupt nature of modern art and society, intended by Lewis as his alternative to Proust and Joyce.

The shift in Lewis's intellectual and artistic position is a reflection of the impact of the Great War. Before the war, the avant-garde was able to attack the bourgeoisie as a class for it stuffiness, commercialism, lack of education and sensibility, and for its inability to live in freedom. After the war, the need to attack the bourgeoisie seemed to have vanished. It was hardly necessary to destabilize the capitalist class and its army of managers and bureaucrats, since the rising importance of socialism throughout Europe and, in particular, the triumphant Bolshevik Revolution of 1917 indicated that the ruling class was under threat from more than mere artists – artists who in any case frequently grew out of that class or at least needed its patronage to survive.

The first issue of *Blast* (June 1914) was an attempt to launch an avant-garde in London imitating the rhetoric of the manifestos of Guillaume Apollinaire in Paris and F. T. Marinetti in Milan. The issue was edited by Lewis, who also provided much of the editorial content. It launched a movement called Vorticism intended to unite avant-garde currents in literature and the visual arts, and featured written contributions from Pound, Ford Madox Hueffer (later Ford Madox

Ford) and Rebecca West, and illustrations from Edward Wadsworth, Frederick Etchells, Jacob Epstein and Gaudier-Brzeska. Except in Lewis's own writing, no Vorticist literature ever came into being, while the visual artists temporarily united as Vorticists would all soon go their separate ways. So in effect, *Blast* represents a moment rather than a movement, and it is dominated by Lewis's agenda. It is no less interesting for that.

The first editorial page of *Blast* rhetorically opposes the individual and artist to the collective society. *Blast* will be anti-bourgeois but not pro-worker:

> Blast will be popular, essentially. It will not appeal to any particular class, but to the fundamental and popular instincts in every class and description of people, TO THE INDIVIDUAL. The moment a man feels or realizes himself as an artist, he ceases to belong to any milieu or time. Blast is created for this timeless, fundamental Artist that exists in everybody.
>
> The Man in the Street and the Gentleman are equally ignored.
> [. . .]
> Blast presents an art of individuals.[2]

The stance of *Blast* is to assert that the artist is independent of class. On the one hand this expresses a desire to be independent of the ruling-class 'Gentleman', on the other a refusal to identify with the working-class or lower middle-class 'Man in the Street'. These terms suggest that artists wish to be unlike any existing social types, and should not make a point of accentuating their wealth and privilege or their poverty by imitating the manners and dress of either class. The point that artists should consider themselves to be independent of the rest of society is a familiar one, inherited from Romanticism. The specific inflection – that the artist should be independent of social class – has a particular resonance in the context of the late 1910s, when the industrial world seemed to be shaping up for a confrontation between capitalism and socialism. The artist was faced with the question of whether to continue to identify with wealth and privilege, or whether, albeit without renouncing wealth and privilege, to identify with the cause of socialism and the common man or woman. In the same way as Joyce asks in *A Portrait of the Artist* and *Ulysses* whether art, or indeed any force, can be independent of the two great forces of imperialism and nationalism, Lewis asks, in 1914, whether the artist can be independent of the great historical forces of capitalism and communism. The intention to map out an independent, classless position of art is abstracted into a model in which opposing class forces are seen as merely mechanical, Newtonian entities. The artist participates in the struggle but has no commitment to either side, as the Vorticist 'Manifesto' declares:

1. Beyond Action and reaction we would establish ourselves.
[. . .]
4. We fight first on one side, then on the other, but always for the SAME cause, which is neither side or both sides and ours.[3]

Lewis's intellectual world was a complex one which only increased in complexity with the passage of time. Yet the stance of *Blast* was strident, intended to strike a clear-cut pose, and its self-conscious avant-gardism is quite different in kind from the symbolism and hermetic, self-reflexive modernism of writers such as Eliot, Virginia Woolf and Joyce, whose point of departure was aestheticism and the esoteric symbolism of the French poet, Stéphane Mallarmé. The presentation of *Blast* is itself remarkable, modelled as it is on manifestos by Apollinaire and Marinetti. It is a large-format publication with a puce cover, and the typesetter has made use of the large page size to set out the 'Manifesto' and other key documents in large, bold type of varying sizes. The object of this presentation is to suggest a kind of confrontation between artists and the general society. At the same time, the strategy of presenting the artist as an individual character-ized by assertions in large, bold type is seen by Lewis, even as early as *Blast*, as being not so much out of step with mass society as in line with it. In the second and final issue of *Blast*, published after the beginning of the war, Lewis ruefully noted that 'THE NEWSPAPERS already smell carrion. They have allowed themselves almost BLAST type already.'[4] Historical events could out-blast anything which artists could produce, and the rapidly growing mass media could use the techniques which *Blast* had used for entirely different purposes.

The early, avant-garde Lewis can be considered a vitalist or a Nietzschean. Vitalism was really the last version of Romantic culture to influence the arts before a backlash against Romanticism in gen-eral began after World War I. The French philosopher Henri Bergson

(1859–1941), who had celebrated the *élan vital*, was an important influence in this regard. The early German romantic Johann Gottlieb Fichte (1762–1814) had responded to Immanuel Kant's philosophy by asserting the importance of self-consciousness and the self-positing nature of the I. Fichte was probably not a direct source for our modernists, but his work in turn created the grounds of possibility for Schopenhauer and Nietzsche, who asserted the primacy of the will, and before them for Max Stirner, whose philosophy of egoism was so extensively criticized by Karl Marx and Friedrich Engels in *The German Ideology* (1845). As we mentioned in chapter 3, there was a brief vogue among modern literati for the ideas of Stirner when his work was published in English translation as *The Ego and his Own* in 1912. Dora Marsden's journal the *Egoist* received contributions from Lawrence, Pound, Eliot, Joyce and Lewis, all at early stages in their careers.

The *Egoist* appropriately published two major works of fiction dealing with the art and the artist, Joyce's *A Portrait of the Artist as a Young Man*, which was serialized in 1914–15, and Wyndham Lewis's *Tarr*, serialized in 1916–17. The Egoist Press published *Portrait* in London as a book dated 1917 (in reality 1918, following its New York publication in 1916) and *Tarr* in 1918. Although each of the writers associated with the *Egoist* had a distinct agenda, while even Dora Marsden was by no means a simple disciple of Stirner, the convergence of disparate individuals around 'egoism' reminds us how significant the theme of the artist's difference from and relationship to society is at this time. It seems hard to define art as anything other than the product of the process of the individual defining himself or herself against society. Joyce's *Portrait* and Lewis's *Tarr* are very different manifestations of this literary tendency.

Tarr (an anagram of ar[r]t) does not seem to be conceived as a direct answer to *Portrait*, although it could be read as a response to Joyce's work, and a detailed account of the parallel would be a fruitful one. Space does not permit that here. However, we should note that Lewis eventually came to see himself as the aesthetic opponent of every current in the literary modernism that would develop over the next decade or so, and that Joyce would become a principal ideological target for him, as evidenced by his attack on Joyce in *Time and Western Man*. Though it was mostly a one-sided conflict, Joyce did incorporate reference to Lewis's criticism into *Finnegans Wake* (serialised as 'Work in progress' in the journal *transition* from 1927 to 1938; book publication, 1939).

In the 1920s Lewis conducted a war against what he saw as the ideological obsession with time of capitalism itself, an obsession shared by mass culture, by philosophy, and by the modernist literature and culture of the elite. *Tarr* was not originally part of this war, although the version I discuss here was revised by Lewis in the 1920s and includes material which reflects that later agenda. Interested readers may compare the 1918 and 1928 versions to establish which passages have been changed.

The most striking thing about *Tarr* on first acquaintance is its style. This represents an attempt by Lewis to produce a Vorticist prose; that is, a literary style which would in some way match the angular avant-gardism of Vorticism in painting and sculpture. In the first version of the novel the prose features the use of the mathematical 'equals' sign (=) as a form of punctuation, designed to break the flow of the text and create a static quality. The idea of a static and painting-like prose is very striking, but Lewis eliminated this device from the second version, presumably regarding it as a distraction. The second version still contains passages of Vorticist-style prose, in the form of deliberately overextended similes, and metaphors designed to foreground the artifice of the text:

> Tarr felt the street was a pleasant current, setting from some immense and tropic gulf, neighboured by Floridas of remote invasions: he ambled down it puissantly, shoulders shaped like these waves, a heavy-sided drunken fish. The houses, with winks of the soft clock-work, were grazed, holding along their surface a thick nap of soft warmth.[5]

We can compare this rendition of a man moving down a city street to the contemplative images of a city in Eliot's 'Preludes' (first published in *Blast*). Eliot's work concentrates on the difference between the subject and the object much as Lewis's does. By this I mean that it is focused on the fact that the internal state and the external world are always different from each other: 'You had such a vision of the street / As the street hardly understands.' These and other lines in 'Preludes' suggest that the difference between inner and outer states is charac-terized by pathos. In fact this pathos is a permanent feature of Eliot's work and recurs in other of his modernist contemporaries. The work of the poet is not to restore the connection between the inner and the outer, but to conjure phrases and images which make the painful difference of the self from the rest of the world all the more acute and laden with pathos. This approach, which concentrates on the relationship between external images and internal states, and more precisely on the discrepancy between images and moods, is influenced by Romanticism in general, in particular by Symbolism. Lewis's approach is in stark contrast to this inner-oriented method, implying a writer not as a suffering subject, but as an active manipulator and sculptor of the raw materials of language.

Tarr is very much a novel of two parts. As originally conceived, the character Tarr was not part of the narrative which came to carry his name. The story was focused on the figure of Otto Kreisler, an artist as Tarr is. The character of Tarr was created at a late stage in the development of the work to accommodate Lewis's desire to offer his own current views on art. Having originally intended to add essays to his book, in the end Lewis added the figure of Tarr, who, though he acts as a mouthpiece for the author, is not able to transcend the world of the other characters. While an author can appear to stand above his characters, the author-character is immanently part of the same world, as 'fallen' as any one else.

The dual genesis of *Tarr* creates a novel with two centres. On the one hand there is the artist Kreisler, a study in the psychology of paranoia and social maladaptation. On the other, there is the aloof artist Tarr, as much a would-be modernist as Kreisler would appear to be a Romantic. These are two poles in the novel which do not quite add up to a whole. Since Tarr is evidently the author's mouthpiece, the judgements which he makes about the meaning of Kreisler's story – a harsh comedy of rejection in love, a duel and suicide – would appear to be authoritative and final. Since we know that so much of what Tarr says reflects the author's opinions, it is difficult not to read the whole novel through his pronouncements:

> This is my theory. I believe that all the fuss he made was an attempt to get out of Art back into Life again. He was like a fish floundering about who had got out of the wrong tank. *Back into sex* I think would describe where he wanted to get to: he was doing his best to get back into sex again out of the little puddle of art where he felt he was gradually expiring.[6]

This vocabulary, describing the failure of an artist who believes that art is a living extension of life rather than the hard, objective antithesis of life, is the common currency of Tarr's many disquisitions in the novel and reflects the author's own vocabulary and preoccupations. However, to read the novel through this statement leads us to ignore the way that the story of Kreisler is set up carefully as an entity in its own right, independent of the concerns with art and art theory which preoccupy Tarr.

Reviewers were quick to comment that the portrayal of Kreisler was indebted to Dostoevsky, whose work had made a huge impact in literary circles since *Crime and Punishment* first appeared in Constance Garnett's English translation in 1911. Dostoevsky's penchant for portraying the psychology of a series of moral monsters in his novels is reflected in Lewis's portrayal of the paranoid Kreisler. That Kreisler is pointedly a German, in a novel written during World War I, and specifically a Prussian with a military education, should not lead us to conclude that Lewis is merely mapping a national stereotype (although the blurb writer for one edition of Tarr anachronistically concluded that Kreisler was a portrait of Hitler). In fact, Kreisler's deep-seated insecurity as an artist in the presence of wealthy art patrons reflects some of the facts which we know about the author and his own occasional social difficulties, and we might easily conclude that far from being a satirical portrait, the depiction of Kreisler includes an element of unflinching self-analysis.

Be that as it may, the figure of Kreisler as a modern psychological portrait is a minor masterpiece, and one not diminished by the only partially accurate parallel with Dostoevsky. In the depictions of *Tarr*, Lewis shows an amazing ability to use objective description to reflect the consciousness of his characters. Indeed, a dislike of internalizing psychological portrayal such as is found in Joyce and Woolf came to be increasingly a topic for Lewis's criticism. Consider this sample of his ability to bring out a mental state in a short depiction which crucially relies not on simpler reflection of the facts but on the artist-writer's intervention:

> Just then a church clock began striking the hour. He foreboded it was already ten, but not later. It struck ten, and then eleven. He leapt the hour – the clock seemed rushing with him, in a second, to the more advanced position – without any flurry, quite calmly. Then it struck

twelve. He at once absorbed that further hour as he had the former. He lived an hour as easily and carelessly as he would have lived a second. Could it have gone on striking he would have swallowed, without turning a hair, twenty, thirty strokes.[7]

If the psychological profiling owes something to Dostoevsky, the prose style, with its baroque and gratuitous elaboration of its own trope, is unmistakably late Dickens – the Dickens of *Great Expectations*. This in itself announces a difference between the modernism of Wyndham Lewis and nearly all the alternatives. While Eliot, Joyce and Woolf each invested in the legacy of symbolism, producing hermetic texts with complex formal features, Lewis centred his own version of modernism on the tradition of satire. Certainly, Dickens is a model, while the oeuvres of Dryden and Swift in particular provide him with an example of politically directed satire and the use of literature to enter the public sphere, rather than shelter from it, which Lewis evidently found very congenial.

The satirical mode would be developed by Lewis to great effect in *The Apes of God* – not without controversy, since this impressive prose achievement betrays more than a hint of anti-Semitic conspiracy theory as part of its assault on the cultural elite of 1920s England. Readers of *Tarr*, however, will be less aware of this development of Lewis's baroque prose style into a fully developed satirical mode, but will be keenly conscious of the art-theorizing from the mouth of Frederick Tarr which occupies much of the framing sections of the narrative. These ideas reflect Lewis's own identification with the latest current of post-Impressionist art theory currently being disseminated in England by Lewis's one-time collaborator, Roger Fry. Fry also introduced Woolf to post-Impressionist theory, and the ideas of Lily Briscoe's art in *To the Lighthouse* reflect the priorities established in Fry's writings collected in *Vision and Design* (1920).

The gist of Fry's arguments, which in general reflect the developments in art of Pablo Picasso and Georges Braque, is that art should not be judged as the simple impression of life, by standards of realism and fidelity, but should be understood as a stylized mediation which reflects the artist's creative and synthetic mode of seeing, rather than any approximation to photography. This emphasis on the art and mind of the artist as the creator, rather than the reflector, of reality recalls the concern of Romantic writers with the artist as a sometimes god-like creator or genius, and the corresponding de-emphasis on art as mimetic, as a reflection of things as they are. Neither Fry nor Lewis shows any distinct awareness that he is revisiting a set of claims about the relationship between subject and object in the mind of the artist that can be found in sources now as familiar as William Wordsworth's *Prelude*. This is probably because in the field of the visual arts their immediate context is that of Impressionism and photography, each of which stresses the artist's responsibility for faithfulness to his or her object (and audience). Following the interests of Picasso and Braque, Fry and Lewis both argue for the importance of non-mimetic art forms in societies that had been judged primitive by comparison with the sophisticated naturalism of the ancient Greeks, which, they believed, had set the model for Western art ever since. Now, the art of contemporary Africans and of ancient civilizations, such as that of Egypt, could be evaluated by different criteria, not merely as inadequate realism, but as fully developed forms based on stylization and design. The lesson of these non-Western art forms was that contemporary art could base itself not on mimetic activity but on the volitional interference of the artist. Art becomes the expression of artistic will, in Lewis a notion underpinned by a reading of Nietzsche and Schopenhauer, whose idea of will can be imported to buttress an artistic credo.

Lewis's *Tarr* asserts this general post-Impressionist credo, and develops the opposition between art and life, central to Roger' Fry's essay 'Art and Life' (1917), into a question not merely of aesthetics but of the artistic life in general. So the protagonist Tarr attempts to live by his own aesthetic ideas, producing an opposition between the hard, abstract masculine and the soft, fleshy feminine:

> With most people, who are not artists, all the finer part of their vitality goes into sex if it goes anywhere [. . .]. The artist is he in whom this emotionality normally absorbed by sex is so strong that it claims a newer and more exclusive field of deployment. its first creation is *the Artist* himself. This is a new sort of person: the creative man. [. . .]

> [D]eadness is the first condition of art. The armoured hide of the hippopotamus, the shell of the tortoise, feathers and machinery, you may put in one camp; naked, pulsing and moving of the soft inside of life – along with elasticity of movement and consciousness – that goes in the opposite camp. Deadness is the first condition for art: the second is

absence of soul, in the human and sentimental sense. With the statue the lines and masses are its soul, no restless inflammable ego is imagined for its interior: it has *no inside*: good art must have no inside: that is capital.[8]

These assertions seem decisive, but the reader is aware that Tarr is a fallible character, whose attempt to cut himself off from women and sex is a comic failure. The endeavour to map art onto gender is not the only element at play here. Tarr's view seems in any case to be contradictory. On the one hand, he asserts that the expressive intention of the artistic will is the most important element in the process of artistic production; on the other, he claims that the objectivity of the art object, independent of any 'genius' supposed to have produced it, is the most important element.

Lewis shared with Eliot a liking for anti-Romantic or classicist rhetoric. At the same time, each writer in a different way is still indebted to Romantic theories which focus more on the artist than on art. Lewis and Eliot deal with this legacy quite differently. Wordsworth pondered his calling as a poet, in the light of his disillusionment with human affairs as the ideals of the French Revolution faded; so too, Lewis and Eliot each considered his role as artist and, increasingly, as cultural commentator, in the light of the redoubled disillusionment which they felt after the debacle of World War I, and what they felt to be the ominous resurgence of bloody revolutionary ideas with the Bolshevik Revolution and the rise of socialism. In *Tarr* the pessimism of works such as *The Art of Being Ruled* is present but far more innocent, being still a question of how the artist must live and how she or he must resist the claims of bourgeois sexuality and bourgeois family life. As a wartime novel of pre-war, aesthetic concerns, *Tarr* stands on a fascinating cusp of time.

CHAPTER 6

James Joyce:
Ulysses and Love

It might never have been possible to apply the term 'modernism' to literature in English had it not been for the existence of James Joyce's *Ulysses* (1922). As in the game in which one is challenged not to think of an elephant and promptly does so, *Ulysses* sits at the centre of the notion of modernism and cannot do otherwise, at least from the English-language perspective. Not only is this work so singular and monumental, but its immediate influence so strongly conditioned the works of other modernists, that we can barely imagine what their works would look like had they not had considered exposure to *Ulysses*. T. S. Eliot praised *Ulysses* for introducing what he called the 'mythical method',[1] by which he meant the use of classical or other established literature to give a narrative or symbolic framework to a new literature rooted in the present.

The existence of *Ulysses* evidently gave Eliot the confidence to publish 'The Waste Land' in its final form. Ezra Pound, who had begun to develop the allusive edifice of *The Cantos* as early as 1917, also took courage from Joyce's use of classical literature, and seems to have been so taken with Joyce's use of Homer's *Odyssey* that he used it himself in what eventually became 'Canto I'. Eliot and Pound saw important formal innovations in Joyce which could be applied in the domain of poetry, and their oeuvres are almost unimaginable without Joyce's example. Virginia Woolf, who experimented with form in *Jacob's Room* (1922), and who was already developing the theme of empire and its effect on everyday life, found Joyce so compelling that her own *Mrs Dalloway* (1925) is laced with borrowings at the level of form and content, although it boldly reverses Joyce's focus on a common man in mid-life crisis to focus on an upper-class woman facing the menopause. Wyndham Lewis saw Joyce as the most symptomatic figure of a literary modernism which he opposed, and constructed major works such as *Time and Western Man* (1927) and *The Apes of God* (1930) in part as a response to Joyce.

So it is not merely that *Ulysses* serves as an example of modernism, but that it directly conditioned many of the English-language works which we now regard as fundamental to modernism, especially those of the 1920s, usually seen as the fulminant period of 'high modernism'. We are therefore quite likely to feel that whatever appears before us in this text is typical, even emblematic, of some entity called 'modernism'. I have deliberately avoided the problems that attach to a term such as 'modernism', which proposes an epistemic centre to an intellectual or cultural moment, whether that is regarded as a particular moment of historical time (such as a period of a decade, say), or whether it is understood in a more Hegelian sense as a particular juncture in a process which is not necessarily confined by dates (so Milton or Eminem *might* be defined in some sense as belonging to a modernist moment).

In a way, I am proposing the opposite problem to any concerning the only half-satisfactory notion of modernism, which is that *Ulysses* seems so emblematic of modernism that it is hard to read it as anything other than a canonical, high modernist text, and what that has usually meant is reading it in terms of its complex formal manoeuvres. It has taken a long time for us to understand collectively just what is there in the text of *Ulysses*, but we are closer to the point of being able to determine what it is about than ever. Yet the issue of what it is about has been confused by the corporate agenda-setting of university criticism.

This is to rush ahead of ourselves. What first presents itself – what first presented itself historically to the earliest readers of this text – is an edifice of almost bewildering complexity. We need to remind ourselves in fact that *Ulysses*, in outline at least, is a relatively straightforward text, not only in terms of its narrative, which occupies the space of one day, but also in terms of its modernism, which amounts to a combination of symbolism and third person centre of consciousness narration in the first nine chapters, followed by a variety of textual forms, intended to stretch the boundaries of narrative propriety, in the last nine chapters. Although it would be possible to emphasize the startling modernity of the range of methods which Joyce develops in this text, and while it would certainly be possible to apply to these pages some loosely theorized notion of the death of the author in a newly decentred textuality (following the terminology of Roland Barthes: see below, chapter 10), it is equally possible to regard the textual devices of *Ulysses* not as a sublime affront to our otherwise normative sense of the world, but as a means of extending the enjoyability of reading. In short, what can be seen as the daring modernism of *Ulysses* is also, simply, its excellence as writing, as a captivating, bravura performance. Or, the writing remains the medium for a content which is basically as determinable as it would be in any more straightforward text.

In other words, the modern reader of *Ulysses* will be looking now more at its meaning or bearing than at its amazing formal properties. However, these formal properties are part of its way of meaning and there is no real escape from the concatenated circle which constitutes *Ulysses'* way of being.

I have set up this discussion on *Ulysses* broadly in terms of form and content, and suggested that the two constitute a kind of circle. I prefer not to discuss this text mainly in terms of its formal features; at the same time, I would encourage readers of *Ulysses* not to fall too directly into a content-based interpretation in which a simple (and usually contemporary) value is urged as the straightforward foundation of the work. Critical fashion has tended to claim that the work is a celebration of the body against the mind or of the vernacular/everyday against the written.[2] Very often the basis of this reading is the assumption that the values of Stephen Dedalus (the central character of *A Portrait of the Artist as Young Man* [1914–15], and an autobiographical version of the young Joyce) are trumped and transcended by those of the protagonist, Leopold Bloom. This is sometimes reinforced by the idea that, much as Bloom's physicality overcomes Stephen's mental abstraction, so too the powerful appearance of Molly Bloom in the final chapter of the novel asserts the physical actuality of femininity over all male logics, whether that of the autodidact Bloom or the Jesuit-trained Dedalus.

Broadly, two claims about *Ulysses* can be asserted against implicit and explicit critical consensus. One, that it is a pessimistic rather than an optimistic work. Two, that it does not declare the independence of text from referent, but explores the discrepancy-in-identity of mind and world, of language and materiality.

By emphasizing the pessimism of *Ulysses*, we are able to discern the naturalist temperament of Joyce's work. Naturalism was the literary movement led by Emile Zola (1840–1902). The naturalist novel followed in the steps of the realist novel and aimed for ever greater degrees of realism. Naturalism was interested in fiction as a medium for depicting people not as agents of their own destiny, but as products of their environment. The techniques of the realist and naturalist novel do not query the representational nature of language, and for this reason naturalism is not often regarded as a principal influence on modernism, which seems above all an operation on textuality itself. Yet in a straightforward way, *Ulysses* belongs to the naturalist tradition and in some ways represents its culmination. In its morass of detail, its relentless search for environmental connection, its documentation of the significant and the meaningless, and above all in its microscopic mapping of the building of minds from the shaping reality, *Ulysses* presents as unsentimentalized a version as is possible of the limitations of the human.

It is the over-riding pessimism, of course, which allows for the streak of qualified optimism in *Ulysses*. Although Christianity is the governing religion in the Ireland of *Ulysses*, the novel does not ask us to believe in a redeeming God. Nor does it ask us to believe in a redeeming human nature. The British occupiers of Ireland are there through the exercise of violence, and their Nationalist opponents are portrayed in the novel as violent and stupid. Nor does *Ulysses* ask us to believe in the redemptive love of the family – at least, not quite. Against the background of a reality conditioned by political violence and by sexual automatism, Joyce asks us to consider what place, however limited, love might still take in the world, and what kind of temporary and secular redemption it might be capable of offering.

Love is present as a sociological theme in Joyce, and as an aesthetic one. In 'The Dead' (from *Dubliners*) Joyce had presented a character, Gabriel Conroy, watching his wife on the stairs as she listens to a singer in another room whom he cannot hear:

> He stood still in the gloom of the hall, trying to catch the air that the voice was singing, and gazing up at his wife. There was grace and mystery in her attitude as if she were a symbol of something. He asked himself, what is a woman standing on the stairs in the shadow, listening to distant music, a symbol of. If he were a painter he would paint her in that

attitude. Her blue felt hat would show off the bronze of her hair against the darkness and the dark panels of her skirt would show off the light ones. *Distant Music* he would call the picture if he were a painter.[3]

As if to deepen the remoteness of the music, the singer is said to be out of voice and the song to be an old one, cast in 'the old Irish tonality'. Later Gabriel learns that the song reminds his wife of a boy who once loved her with so much passion that he walked miles in the rain to stand outside her window and consequently died of pneumonia. When he hears this Gabriel feels moved, but also shut out: 'Generous tears filled Gabriel's eyes. He had never felt like that himself towards any woman but he knew that such a feeling must be love' (p. 224). The topic here is the nature and structure of love. It is tackled through the optic of the nature and structure of the aesthetic. Gabriel is a sophisticated, Europeanized aesthete, who can view love in terms of aesthetic experience, but fears he may have missed out on the real, unmediated experience of a genuine passion – here a passion so total that it ends in death.

The 'generous tears' permit a reading of Gabriel as generous or, more likely, as deluded. What is interesting for us here is the way in which the aesthete Gabriel, following in the tracks of the late nineteenth-century Aesthetic Movement associated with Walter Pater and Oscar Wilde, breaks down his experience into visual, aural, verbal, symbolic realms. Joyce demonstrates an interest in the way that experience is brought by senses which are unrelated to each other. On the one hand, there is a common-sense suggestion that what we experience as the world is a unity; on the other hand, we experience the world in sensory fragments which have a life, identity or moment of their own. In the quotation from 'The Dead', Joyce shows that the aesthetic consists not so much of a single impression given to a single sense in one moment of time as of a kind of layering in which (in this case) the heard (the song) is unheard, but captured in the image of the hearer (Gabriel's wife), and where the meaning of the moment is not wholly present to any participant. The vision of his wife on the stairs is not fully present to Gabriel, since she is half in shadow. The song heard by his wife is half heard, since she is not in the room and the singer is not in full voice. Moreover, his wife (as Gabriel learns) is not moved by the content of the song, but by the association she has with it, her memory of her young dead suitor.

What Joyce shows in this passage, then, is that the aesthetic moment is always about some deferred totality, not about some fully present thing. This idea of deferral is important in Joyce, and is one given increased meaning for modern readers of his text by the work of Jacques Derrida (see below, chapter 10).

On the one hand, a series of impressions arriving through the different senses; complex, ever-differentiated surfaces. On the other, the possibility of a binding force. Is the world itself a unity? Is it the understanding which binds together the data of the different senses into some kind of unity? Or is love the force which suggests shape, meaning, purpose in the world?

In the context of 'The Dead' these questions are given a very specific substance; love is connected with the supposedly simple values of old Ireland, the aestheticism of Gabriel with cosmopolitan (and English) sophistication. Moreover, the reader is not given a clear position to examine, as the 'love' which closes Gabriel's vision is itself the many-layered product of his aestheticizing vision – a vision into which, we are told, he 'swoons', a word perhaps used to mock his aesthete's manner of perceiving the world.

In the context of *Ulysses* these matters are considerably broadened. Everything in the arrangement of the work posits a tension between underlying unities and the proliferation and over-layering of meaning. The title of the book suggests this tension. Ulysses appears to be a single figure and a seeming unity, until we recall that Ulysses is in any case the Latin name of Odysseus, suggesting a process of migration of meaning between cultures and languages, rather than any simple unity. Like the *Odyssey*, which provides its skeletal model, *Ulysses* takes place within a circumscribed time and place – in the case of *Ulysses* one day, 16 June 1904, and one city, Dublin. Yet as in Homer's *Odyssey*, although the events take place over one day, they are dominated by the past which is present in various forms to the minds of the participants, and which both consciously and unconsciously determines patterns of action and conduct.

The way in which the past stands over and determines the present is a key theme of this work, not least because occupied Dublin offers a clear-cut example of the past as a violence which intrudes bodily into the present, in the form of the British occupying forces. The presence of the past is announced as a concern of the work in two of the more heavily signposted themes of *Ulysses*, paternity and ghosts. The notion of the ghost is explicitly explored in several of Stephen Dedalus's meditations. Stephen has tried to escape the burden of Irish history by escaping to Paris. He has come crashing down to earth (like Icarus, the son of Dedalus who flew too close to the sun), and his dream of being an aesthete and poet is temporarily grounded. Having returned to Ireland, and to the history which he tried to escape, Stephen finds himself bound by the past in both material and symbolic ways. Materially, his home is usurped by the political indifferentist Mulligan and the Englishman Haines. Symbolically, he is haunted, not least by his failure to respond to his mother's request to kneel at her deathbed – a deference to a parental wish which he is unable to make because it would imply symbolic capitulation to the authority of the church.

In a key early part of the narration, Buck Mulligan, the medical student and materialist, taunts Stephen about his actions at his mother's bedside:

> – You wouldn't kneel down to pray for your mother on her deathbed when she asked you. Why? Because you have the cursed Jesuit strain in you, only it's injected the wrong way. To me its all a mockery and beastly. Her cerebral lobes are not functioning. [. . .] I didn't mean to offend the memory of your mother. [. . .]
> – I am not thinking of the offence to my mother.
> – Of what, then? Buck Mulligan asked.
> – Of the offence to me, Stephen answered. (p. 8)

To Mulligan, who handles bodies as mere bodies, spiritual and symbolic meanings are dismissible. However, as the title of the earlier short story 'The Dead' reminds us, the bodily reality of the human world is constantly haunted by the ghosts of the dead – as words, images, histories – claims which are present to us and make demands on us just as the ghost of Hamlet's father made claims on Hamlet to take revenge.

Ulysses traffics constantly in these ghostly claims. One of the best-known references in the text to the idea of the ghostliness of history comes in the second chapter, 'Nestor', where Stephen is found in his role as a history teacher at a boys' school. In an effectively contrived episode, Stephen is shown unwillingly trying to communicate the facts about the battle of Tarentum to an unreceptive class. After the lesson, he is called in by Mr Deasy, the headmaster of Dalkey School. Deasy is an anti-Semite who believes that history moves towards an end pre-ordained by God. Stephen's belief, to the contrary, seems to be that lives may be assembled in a decentred fashion from heterogeneous elements. However, he acknowledges the power and presence of the past, of a symbolic narrative called 'history':

> – History, Stephen said, is a nightmare from which I am trying to awake. From the playfield the boys raised a shout. A whirring whistle: goal. What if that nightmare gave you a back kick?
> – The ways of the Creator are not our ways, Mr Deasy said. All history moves towards one great goal, the manifestation of God.
> Stephen jerked his thumb towards the window, saying:
> – That is God.
> Hooray! Ay! Whrrwhee!
> – What? Mr Deasy asked.
> – A shout in the street, Stephen answered, shrugging his shoulders.
> (p. 42)

I have quoted the famous line in its context to allow its fullest sense to emerge. Stephen rejects the idea that history moves towards a final goal before Deasy has even stated it. Yet it is also clear to Stephen that it is not adequate to dismiss history as a ghost: a nightmare is a bad dream in which the dreamer feels suffocated by a female spirit or being. Yet history cannot be thought of as a purely symbolic, immaterial entity, since it has consequences in the present – consequences which may be violent, as Stephen acknowledges in his silent self-correction: 'What if that nightmare gave you a back kick?'

We are not allowed to side with Stephen's desire to dismiss history. We already know that he has crashed to earth and returned to Dublin and the history which formed him. Moreover we see in this compactly symbolic episode that Stephen's alternative vision of God is not the final word, although Stephen is well aware that his cosmopolitan sophistication leaves the provincial Deasy standing. Certainly Stephen's remark that God is a 'shout in the street' offers a crisply defined alternative to Deasy's notion that history moves towards a goal – a Judaeo-Christian idea which chimed in with nineteenth-century ideas of progress. Stephen's notion is that 'history' consists not of a constant stream of articulated meaning, but of its opposite, of disarticulated and isolated sounds. Yet this aestheticizing view, which seizes on the moment in which an impression is received – a kind of Imagist moment if we will – is not adequate as a view of reality. The sound heard outside the window is not simply a shout in the street, but a shout which has gone up, mingled with other sounds, from a game of hockey which is being played outside. Though the sound which comes to Stephen is a random-seeming intensity, it nevertheless arises within the framework of a carefully articulated symbolic context – a game. *Ulysses* consistently presents sport as an obsession of Dubliners who, seeking to displace their historical antagonism to the English occupation, divert their hostility into the symbolic competitiveness of sport. Sport is a narrative much like history, and moves towards goals in the same way as Deasy claims that history does.

Is it possible to claim that the present moment has primacy over the claims of history? Is it possible to live in the present? The ghost-like presence of history cannot be easily disregarded or exorcized. In another often-cited line, Stephen says to Deasy: ' I fear those big words [. . .] which make us so unhappy' (p. 38). History is just such a big word, like all big words binding human meanings, and obliging the present to something which lies outside it but haunts it with ghostly claims. Yet another of these big words is love – a big word which *Ulysses* interrogates for whatever possibility it may have to redeem the present in the name of the ghostly. Is love an alternative to history?

In 'The Dead', we saw that love was treated in the context of aestheticism, something endlessly deferred from the present. In *Ulysses* Joyce focuses in both a humanly involved and a sociologically dispassionate way on love in its lived context, that of familial and erotic love. The idea of non-sexual love as advocated by Christianity – and Joyce's text is nothing if not theologically aware – offers the vision of a society in which everyone is tied together harmoniously by disinterested care for the other. This is the vision of love celebrated by socialism, in which the love of familial bonds is displaced on to the whole community. However, for such love to be displaced from the family on to the community – a possibility which Joyce's text seems to doubt – it is necessary for family love, the love of husband and wife and of parent and child, to be the wholesome and disinterested thing which the ideal appears to suggest. Yet the most fundamental bond of love in actually existing society is that between a husband and wife, and this love is one that can only with difficulty be thought of as disinterested, since the bond of marriage is also a sexual one, and sexual love (or *eros*) returns to haunt the more disinterested notion of brotherly love (or *agape*).

Joyce makes erotic love and its possible transmutation into non-sexual love the principle theme of his main plot, which concerns the marriage between Leopold and Molly Bloom, a marriage which has resulted in the birth of a daughter, Milly, but also in the loss of a son, Rudy, a loss which has quietly destroyed the sexual relationship between Leopold and Molly. The central line of the main plot concerns Molly's meeting for sex with her singing partner Blazes Boylan. Although this meeting is kept secret by Molly, Bloom is aware of it and spends the day away from the house, trying to keep his mind off the event as far as possible. In human interest terms, Joyce creates a fascinating scenario, in which Bloom can be seen, much as his model Odysseus, as an anti-hero who avoids direct conflict with his enemies. Yet by declining to confront his wife over her adultery, Bloom successfully maintains his relationship with her. The conclusion of the work, which places Bloom and Molly sleeping in bed together head to toe like a pair of question marks, indeed places a question mark over this limited triumph of love. This ambivalent conclusion, and partial victory of a form of love which is not merely erotic, has to be seen as a limited salvation from erotic love itself, which is viewed in *Ulysses* as a conditioning agent more powerful – even – than the 'history' which has brought the British occupation of Ireland.

The structure of erotic love is one in which the mind of one encounters the body of another. *Ulysses* looks for a meeting of minds but does not find one. The minds of Bloom and Dedalus – symbolic father and son – are left curiously segregated in the key scene ('Eumaeus') where we might expect them to find a unity (just as Odysseus discovers his relationship with his son Telemachus). Moreover, we have seen Bloom's mind separated from that of his wife throughout. They share only the most rudimentary communication, and the final segment of the book ('Penelope') is an astounding stream-of-consciousness monologue in which Molly, who has been present throughout mostly as Bloom's imagined version of her, is now finally given to us in her own isolation, independently of the person of her husband.

It is a commonplace to observe of *Ulysses* that there is a shift from the mental world of Stephen, in the first three chapters, to the concrete, physical, above all bodily world of Bloom in the remainder of the text. From this, it would be easy to conclude that *Ulysses* asserts the primacy of body, especially since each chapter concerning Bloom is known to have a particular part of the body associated with it, and since Bloom is depicted performing a variety of physical functions normally left unrepresented in Victorian fiction – urinating, masturbating and so on.

However, it is more subtle, and more accurate to the work's intentions, to suggest that Joyce is not developing an optimistic vision of the bodily life as the fullest form of life available, but rather the contrary. Joyce examines the role of the mind as the place in which the body takes shape; both one's own body and the bodies of others. Body and mind are united, in that body appears only to and for mind. However, as Joyce shows, each mind is separated from others, and the possibility of the mind properly and truly grasping the body founders on what now appears as the bizarre alienation of sexual difference.

Sexual desire is predicated on the desire of the mind for the body of the other. Sexual desire does not take place in a vacuum, but in a very determinate set of social relations. In the context of *Ulysses*, sexual desire is exclusively heterosexual (with examples of gender inversion, but infrequently of same-sex desire). This does not necessarily reflect authorial predisposition, but rather attempts to reflect the social reality of Dublin in 1904 – a reality in which the sexes are carefully segregated, encountering each other according only to certain rules, with sex itself either taking place within the carefully circumscribed boundaries of marriage, or taking place (or being hinted at) in an equally bounded way outside the confines of marriage (fantasy, voyeurism, exhibitionism, flirtation, adultery). The social situation of sexuality is one of alienation, and Joyce's text provides a very specific map of the manner in which this alienation is rooted both in social particularity (the social and sexual mores of Dublin) and in the alienation of mind from body.

Joyce's mapping of the issue is both sociological and what I have called theological, the latter in that it pertains to the problem of thinking through or realizing one's own proper being and the being of others. These issues are depicted to remarkable effect in one of the most noted chapters of *Ulysses*, 'Sirens'. The first impact of 'Sirens' on any reader is its sheer formal difficulty and bravura. The theme of the chapter is music, and the prose is styled to recall music in many of its details, while the overall shaping of the narrative is intended to mimic the musical device of counterpoint, in which different musical (or in this case narrative) lines are heard simultaneously in differing degrees of prominence. Beneath this glistening surface, however, there is a relatively straightforward narrative thread, part of which concerns the two barmaids in the Ormond Bar where Bloom and another group of men are taking a drink. I want to focus here on these two barmaids.

It would be easy enough to take this chapter as a celebration of Irish vernacular culture, the common culture of drink and song as opposed to the high culture of mind and books which it is sometimes felt Joyce places second to the common life. However, it is more likely that Joyce's naturalistic eye has chosen the bar as a site of the enactment of social and sexual alienation in one of its profoundest forms. The 'Sirens' of the chapter's title (which does not appear in most editions; Joyce supplied the chapter titles subsequently) are the barmaids, who correspond to the Homeric Sirens whose song created such a yearning in men that they sailed their ships onto the rocks and were destroyed. If Homer's framework is epic and heroic, Joyce's version is, as ever, quotidian and banal, and migrates from his model in Homer to suggest a wholly different series of meanings about the nature of everyday life in the modern world. The barmaids are the only women in the bar, which is frequented exclusively by men. It would, presumably, have been considered improper for a married woman to work in a bar, since part of these women's role is to provide a sexualized lure to male drinkers with whom they are obliged to flirt. Sexuality here is mediated by the economics of the bar, the parties are unequal, and the alienation extends to both sides, as Joyce clearly shows, since desire on neither side can be realized. Instead of a unifying and transcendent love – the ideal love which may perhaps have no real place in the world – we witness a scene of melancholy and bluster in which desire is displaced into flirtation and fetishism.

This notion of fetishism is a key component in Joyce's mapping of the working of desire. Throughout the novel Bloom is depicted as having a fetish for women's underwear. Molly Bloom sneers at this in her closing monologue in 'Penelope', but at the same time reveals that she sees herself and other women in terms of the fetishization of clothing, especially of underwear, and in that of non-sexual parts of the body. Joyce is, I think, aware that even the sexual parts of the body are also fetishized in desire. On this view, the penis or vagina is not the *authentic* object of desire defined against supposedly *inauthentic* objects, such as the foot or shoe. Rather, even the sexual parts are fetishistic objects of desire in the sense that they are parts detached from an elusive whole. Desire latches on to isolated aspects of the physical presence of the other in search for completion, perhaps in the form of a master narrative called 'love'. This holistic love is elusive, and it may be the nature of desire that no individual can really fulfil it, since any individual or any body part can just as easily be substituted, in the desiring mind, for another.

We recall here Gabriel Conroy's experience of love in 'The Dead' as something which hovers elusively behind a series of sense impressions. In *Ulysses*, Joyce takes his analysis out of the framework of Conroy's aestheticism and applies it to a more naturalistically modelled version of sexuality. So in the Ormond Bar we witness the snapping of the garter as the moment in which the alienation of sexuality is as fully presented in the text as love is elusively absent from real life. 'Aren't men frightful idiots?', exclaims Miss Douce early in the chapter (p. 331), as a man passing looks back at her, presumably ogling. The text immediately qualifies that she makes this exclamation, which we might take as a confident rebuttal of the folly of male sexuality, 'With sadness'. Although these barmaids reject male attention, they are also quietly unhappy that they are unmarried, and that sexuality takes this course – of ogling, flirtation and so on – a game that each side must play to the point that the women, who actually would like to be married, must pretend to mock these informal and malfunctioning institutions of courtship as part of the game, pretending not to be interested. This sadness is important for us to note since it indicates the nature of the tone of melancholy, rather than of celebration or affirmation, which pervades much of this text; a melancholy that alienated life is not what it might be. Shortly afterwards, the men in the bar beg Miss Douce to sound the time (*'Sonnez la cloche!'*), by which it transpires they mean that she should snap her garter by way of giving them a flirtatious thrill. Joyce creates this scene with great refinement. This is evidently a ritual, something Miss Douce has done before, since the request is not met with surprise and requires no elaboration. Miss Douce waits until her co-worker Miss Kennedy is out of earshot, because part of the game is that such improper things, which women must do to interest men, must not be done in the presence of other women, who would be obliged to disapprove:

> Bending, she nipped a peak of skirt above her knee. Delayed. Taunted them still, bending, suspending, with wilful eyes.
> – *Sonnez!*
> Smack. She let free sudden in rebound her nipped elastic garter smackwarm against her smackable woman's warmhosed thigh. (p. 343)

Why do these men want to hear the garter snap? And why does Miss Douce want to let them hear? Everything points to sex, but sex is displaced. Even to show her knee is highly provocative behaviour in the context of 1904 Dublin (as Molly reveals in her own extensive meditations on women's flirtation in 'Penelope'). To show the garter is out of the question, but to hear it is another displaced satisfaction. What the men hear is both the sound of the fetishized piece of underwear, and the sound of the fleshy leg against which it snaps, and they are reminded of the warmth of her thigh which they would feel if they had intercourse with her, and of the sound and feel of their own bodies smacking against her. Perhaps they are also reminded of the warmth of her vagina, though the text does not state as much. The vagina, more so than the penis, is both the centre of love and yet a strange absence, for all that male desire aims towards it. Molly in her final monologue reveals that she is unfulfilled by Boylan, despite the size of his penis, and it is Molly who in her unselfconscious articulacy most closely names this mystery by which love is deferred through the fetishized layering of the structure of sexuality: 'whats the idea making us like that with a big hole in the middle of us' (p. 877). 'Hole' puns on 'whole' and the elusive nature of fulfilment, which cannot be achieved merely by being filled.

How can love fulfil its promise of fulfilled being? Joyce knows well that Christianity and its modern secular form, socialism, make the promise of redeeming the world by a love which will transcend sexuality and particular interest. He makes Bloom the spokesman of both love and socialism, in an equivocal manner which suggests the severe limitation of the secularized notion of love despite its evident theological promise. In 'Cyclops', Bloom famously confronts the hateful nationalism and anti-Semitism of a figure called 'the Citizen' with a speech about love:

– But it's no use, says he. Force, hatred, history, all that. That's not life
for men and women, insult and hatred. And everybody knows that it's
the very opposite of that that is really life.
– What? Says Alf.
– Love, says Bloom. I mean the opposite of hatred. I must go now.
(p. 432)

Bloom is equated with Christ in a manner that is only partly satirical;
Christ too announced a doctrine of love and was obliged to depart
abruptly. Yet the content of Bloom's socialist theory of secularized love
is given only comic articulation when he makes a speech about it in
'Circe', the chapter in which the darker side of human realities appears:

I stand for the reform of municipal morals and the plain ten command-
ments. New worlds for all. Union of all, jew, moslem and gentile.
Three acres and a cow for all children of nature. Saloon motor hearses.
Compulsory manual labour for all. All parks open to the public day and
night. Electric dishscrubbers. Tuberculosis, lunacy, war and mendacity
must now cease. General amnesty, weekly carnival, with masked
licence, bonuses for all, Esperanto the universal brotherhood. No more
patriotism of barspongers and dropsical impostors. Free money, free
love and a free lay church in a free lay state. (p. 610)

This wonderful passage weaves together the demands made at this
time by all manner of socialists, reformers and free-love idealists. As if
saloon motor hearses could affect the nature of death! It concludes
comically with a coded focus on the ideal of sexual love which we
have discussed – the ideal of universal love is here brought down, by
a seemingly accidental form of words, to the mere desire for a 'free
lay' – a purely pleasureful existence in the present, beyond the claims
of society and history.

What I have suggested is the pessimism of *Ulysses*, or rather its limited
optimism, is carefully and lightly marked out here in this delicate
satire on the actual forms which the desire to transcend existing
society have adopted in the minds of many, and, here, in the mind of
the limited and equivocal embodiment of the ideal of secularized love
which is Joyce's protagonist, Leopold Bloom.

CHAPTER 7

D. H. Lawrence: Jazz and Life

In his poetry collection *The Weary Blues* (1926), the African American poet Langston Hughes demonstrated the potential of adapting the ethos and feel of blues and jazz to a new form of 'Negro' modernism which would permit expression not only to the reality explored in Alain Locke's anthology *The New Negro* (1925), but to the new and emerging realities of multiracial America, at this time popularly conceived in terms of the 'melting pot' of races. Hughes was part of a large and shifting group of African American writers and artists active in the 1920s, based mainly in New York, whose activities are known to history as the Harlem Renaissance. While the periodization of American culture at this time is unusually portentous (this 'Renaissance' of a decade or so takes its place alongside a 'Jazz Age' and a 'Swing Era' of similarly brief duration), such vocabulary at least reinforces the sense that American modernity was undergoing rapid developments which to many felt epochal, in relation both to African American culture and to American culture as a whole.

> Droning a drowsy syncopated tune,
> Rocking back and forth to a mellow croon,
> I heard a Negro play.[1]

Though Hughes's poem, 'Weary Blues', is rhymed, it draws on the liberties of free verse in seeking to incorporate the feeling of African American speech idiom and the particular rhythmic flexibility of the irregular pace of rural blues.

The Harlem Renaissance poets and novelists enjoyed a vogue for all things Negro in America and Europe which cut both ways. The African American artist had an audience which included whites and blacks, and attempting to please and integrate with liberal whites proved an uncomfortable compromise against the background of African American political opinion, which was divided as to the virtues of integration, and which included a separatist lobby which pointed to the risks of offering a primitive version of the Negro to a white audience conditioned by decades of racial ideology. The division ran deep between African Americans who sought middle-class status and respectability, on the one hand, and those who resisted the American ideology of self-help, on the other. Langston Hughes lambasted the compromised, middle-class Negro intellectual in his 1926 essay, 'The Negro Artist and the Racial Mountain':

> So I am ashamed for the black poet who says, 'I want to be a poet, not a Negro poet', as though his own racial world were not as interesting as any other world. I am ashamed, too, for the colored artist who runs from the painting of Negro faces to the painting of sunsets after the manner of the white academicians because he fears the strange un-whiteness of his own features. [...]
> Let the blare of Negro jazz bands and the bellowing voice of Bessie Smith singing Blues penetrate the closed ears of the colored near-intellectual until they listen and perhaps understand. [...] We younger Negro artists who create now intend to express our individual dark-skinned selves without fear or shame. If white people are pleased we are glad. If they are not, it doesn't matter. We know we are beautiful. And ugly too. The tom-tom cries and the tom-tom laughs. If colored people are pleased we are glad. If they are not, their displeasure doesn't matter either. We build our temples for tomorrow.[2]

Hughes reprimands Negro intellectuals for their disdain for regarding existing African American culture – jazz and blues – as primitive (they reject it as 'blare' and 'bellowing'). At the same time, he clearly signals an anxiety about pleasing both black and white audiences, either of which might reject the new black art for failing to correspond, on the one hand, to clichés of negritude or, on the other, to sanctioned European models. Hughes insists on the independence of the artist just as European avant-gardists had done.

On a visit to the USA in 1927, Wyndham Lewis caught sight of the new interest in negritude among both black and white writers. Lewis was a keen observer of the manner in which, as he thought, elements of high-brow and popular culture operated as the ideological advocates of industrial domination, and of a form of cultural standardization and economic integration which we would now call globalization. In *Paleface: The Philosophy of the 'Melting-Pot'* (1929) he presented a sequence of essays in which he offered a critique of several writers of the Renaissance, as well as an extended assault on the primitivism of Sherwood Anderson and D. H. Lawrence. Lewis seizes on W. E. B. Du Bois' novel *Dark Princess* (1928), a political fantasy concerning the future of the African American in world political history. Lewis seems not to know of Du Bois' importance in the National Association for the Advancement of Colored People; nor is he aware that Du Bois uses this novel to criticize the idea of a simple inversion of racial power and to assert the validity of socialist democracy. Lewis's account of this book is an interesting piece of misprision. He highlights what he mistakenly takes to be Du Bois' attempt to present whiteness as the marginalized other of blackness, quoting a passage in which the protagonist, a young black doctor, disillusioned with the white world that regulates his existence, is suddenly reconfirmed in his blackness by the sight of a beautiful black woman: 'First and above all came that sense of color: into this world of pale yellowish and pinkish parchment, that absence or negation of color, came suddenly a glow of brown skin.'[3] The novel plots a political conspiracy by a group representing the 'non-white races', led by the 'dark princess' of the title. Lewis, perhaps on the basis of reading only the first few chapters, claims that, in this novel, 'the Coloured Peoples are urged to develop a consciousness of *superiority* and the same book seeks to force upon the Paleface a corresponding sense of *inferiority*' (p. 41). Had Lewis read to the end, he would have found that Du Bois rejects 'a world wide war of dark against white will', preferring the ideal of 'the world-wide abolition of the color-line.'[4]

Lewis briefly discusses Harlem Renaissance authors Nella Larsen and Alain Locke, but his main focus is on the romanticization of blackness, the primitive and the unconscious in the works of such authors as Lawrence and Sherwood Anderson. Lewis makes rather a lot of a small number of works, principally Anderson's *Dark Laughter* (1925) and Lawrence's *Mornings in Mexico* (1927). Lewis's approach is dogmatically bent on proving his conclusion: that whites are abandoning their culture and succumbing to their own romantic myth of the primitive, in the process creating their own 'inferiority complex', since they are no longer in touch with outer or inner nature, as they believe the non-white races to be:

> So, in the books that we have been considering, where the White Man is confronted by the Black, the Red or the Brown, he now feels inside himself a novel sensation of *inferiority*. He has, in short, an 'inferiority complex' where every non-White, or simply alien personality or consciousness, is concerned. Especially as it is in his capacity of *civilized* (as opposed to *primitive*, 'savage,' 'animal') that he has been taught to feel *inferior*. (p. 240)

No one will, I think, concede Lewis anything like the last word on this topic, but his work is interesting in that it attempts to seize, concretize and make available for critique the impact of African American culture (and of the racial other in general) as it is received and transformed in the white industrial world. It confirms, as we might perhaps expect, that, in the European context, jazz and negritude had become mapped on to the concerns of Romanticism and its aftermath, just as they had in the USA.

It is clear that little of the complexity of the social situation of African Americans had registered strongly with European writers and thinkers. The over-riding impact of African American culture in Europe was not literary but musical, in the form of ragtime and jazz. Eliot seems to mock the histrionic regard for this music in 'The Waste Land':

> O O O O that Shakespeherian Rag –
> It's so elegant
> So intelligent.[5]

Though Eliot seems to have enjoyed popular music, these lines appear to be among those in his work which characterize others as turning aside from suffering interiority and having recourse instead to a mask of mechanical, external expression, like the typist who 'puts a record on the gramophone'.

The connection with the gramophone is material for jazz, since ragtime and jazz spread through Europe in large part via the medium of the gramophone. The 'automatic hand' of Eliot's typist, smoothing her hair, reminds us that many at this time believed that jazz music and jazz dance were basically mechanical – a reflection in music of the domination of modern society by the machine, at a time when machines harnessed human bodies *en masse* to their own rhythms of mechanized mass production.

To the modern reader this may seem strange, since for us jazz is associated not with mechanical expression but rather with its opposite, with the lability of modern jazz's swing and with the apparently limitless possibilities of individual self-expression in the jazz solo. We should remind ourselves, though, that swing and the jazz solo are components of jazz which, though they came to dominate modern jazz, were still under development in the forms of jazz heard in the 1920s. Certainly, Louis Armstrong could be heard on record from 1925 with his famous Hot Five and Hot Seven. While Armstrong as a soloist clearly has a fully developed notion of swing as a component of an approach to soloing of breathtaking richness and virtuosity, it is also plain that his musical associates do not swing and, despite their undoubted quality of musicianship, do not reach the heights of emotional expressivity which Armstrong unveils wholesale on side after amazing side.

What this reminds us is that the expressive potential of swing and the jazz solo was something that had to be invented, and was by no means a universal characteristic of the music of this period. What European ears heard as jazz is better represented by the responses of European composers of concert music to jazz. Stravinsky's theatre piece *The Soldier's Tale* (1918) is a benchmark in this regard. It is scored for seven musicians, including clarinet, bassoon, cornet, trombone and percussion, and its acid sonorities and frequent march times refract the jazz of its time through Stravinsky's own compositional framework. In Germany, Hindemith's Kammermusik No. 1 (op. 24 no. 1: 1921 was scored for 12 musicians, among them clarinet, bassoon, trumpet, accordion, xylophone, and percussion including a siren and a sand-filled tin can. Again, this piece is characterized by acidic harmonies and strident and lively rhythms which seem to turn their back on the pre-war ideal of concert music as the public expression of deep internal emotion. This is one of the pieces excoriated by Theodor Adorno (see below, chapter 9) in an early piece on 'utility music', which he accuses of rejecting interiority in the name of an exteriority which strives to make itself object-like and in doing so merely accords with the tendency of modern society to make subjects into objects.[6]

Adorno later commented on the 'bizzarerie of frenzied but shrill asphalt-harmonies' in jazz that they did not represent 'big city degeneration, a rootless exoticism, certainly not in the way that innocents think'. Nor did it 'have to do with real Negro music, which here a long time ago became industrially smoothed out and faked'. Adorno claimed that jazz as transmitted though Europe and recently banned by the Nazis was 'the utility music of the high bourgeois upper stratum in the post war period', a safe way to encounter musical modernity.[7] Adorno went on in later pieces to theorize the manner in which jazz participated in the harnessing of the body and psyche by the rationalizing forces of industrial production.[8]

Where jazz occurs in Lawrence's work, it is also in the context of its impact on the upper classes in terms of its effect on mind and body and the possibility of an authentic existence. In Lawrence and Adorno, this take on jazz as a part of industrial modernity, and its location by each writer in terms of (otherwise differing) speculative ontological critique, is evidently far removed from the debates of the writers of the Harlem Renaissance for whom jazz embodied, conflictually, modern expressive possibility and primitive myth.

Lady Chatterley's Lover (1928) is not of course a novel about jazz. References to jazz are occasional and apparently cursory. Yet it is a novel about the jazz age, one which adopts quite a different tack from Scott Fitzgerald's *The Great Gatsby* (1925), and, closer to home, Michael Arlen's *The Green Hat* (1924), the less well-known English 'jazz age' novel. Lawrence leads us to understand that jazz has become a part of everyday life for workers and upper class alike. For the workers, jazz dance is seen as an unhopeful supplement to their working life:

> The colliers aren't pagan – far from it. They're a sad lot, a deadened lot of men: dead to their women, dead to life. The young ones scoot about on motor-bikes with girls, and jazz when they get a chance. But they're very dead.[9]

Here it is Mellors who speaks. In the words of another surrogate for authorial analysis, Tommy Dukes, jazz is connected to the body shape which became popular in the 1920s, the slim, flat, androgynous look:

> Personally I consider bolshevism half-witted. But so I consider our social life in the west: half-witted. We're all as cold as cretins: we're all as passionless as idiots. – We're all of us bolshevists – only we give it another name. [. . .] Love's another of those half-witted performances, today. Fellows with swaying waists fucking little jazz girls with small boy buttocks like two collar-studs? Do you mean that sort of love? (p. 39)

In fact the narrative of the novel describes Constance Chatterley's transition from having just such a body to the fullness and roundedness of the sexually satisfied person she becomes through her relationship with the gamekeeper, Mellors. As the quoted passages testify, jazz is not associated with vitality, as *Paleface* might lead us to expect, but with the very opposite, deadness and mechanism. Tommy Dukes finds both communism and modern sexuality passionless, just as Mellors finds the working men 'dead'.

Jazz is also seen as part of a 'sophisticated' life of parties and flirting which offers simple narcosis in a culture of 'enjoyment' that lacks authenticity, as Connie finds when her sister takes her away from England to the Venice Lido:

> It was pleasant in a way. It was *almost* enjoyment. But anyhow, with all the cocktails, all the lying in warmish water and sun-bathing on hot sand in hot sun, jazzing with your stomach up against some fellow in warm nights, cooling off with ices, it was a complete narcotic. And that was what they all wanted, a drug: the slow water, a drug; jazz, a drug; cigarettes, cocktails, ices, vermouth – To be drugged! Enjoyment! Enjoyment! (p. 259)

Here jazz appears not as a primitive reversion to authentic sexuality but as its opposite, as part of a sophisticated hedonism comparable to that of Scott Fitzgerald's fictional world, in which the lack of authentic being is narcotically eclipsed.

By contrast to this, in a key scene, Constance Chatterley looks at herself in the mirror and compares her body to the contemporary 'flapper' standard:

She was supposed to have a good figure, but now she was out of fashion: a little too female, not enough like an adolescent boy. [...] Instead of ripening its firm, down-running curves, her body was flattening and going a little harsh. It was is if it had not had enough sun and warmth. It was a little greyish and sapless. Disappointed of its real womanhood, it had not succeeded in becoming boyish and unsubstantial and transparent. (p. 70)

Constance's body tends to an androgyny which does not suit it. Lawrence allows us to infer that a full, feminine ripeness is more proper for Connie and, by extension, for all women. Connie's upbringing is described in the opening pages of the book as being that of the most sophisticated liberal upper class of that time. Her mother is a Fabian socialist, her father an artist, and they have sought to broaden her mind by an 'aesthetically unconventional upbringing' involving much travel abroad and attendance at 'great socialist conventions' (p. 6). Her background is bohemian and liberated. She and her sister have been led to regard themselves as the equals if not superiors of men, and their most valued relationship with men is verbal – sex is a mechanical second:

Both Hilda and Constance had had their tentative love affairs, by the time they were eighteen. The young men with whom they talked so passionately and sang so lustily and camped under the trees in such freedom wanted, of course, the love-connection. [...] And however one might sentimentalise it, this sex business was one of the most ancient sordid connections and subjections. Poets who glorified it were mostly men. Women had always known there was something higher. And now they knew it more definitely than ever. The beautiful pure freedom of a woman was infinitely more wonderful than any sexual love. [...] A woman could take a man without giving herself away. Certainly she could take herself without giving herself into his power. Rather she could use this sex thing to have power over him. For she had only to hold herself back, in the sexual intercourse, and let him finish and expend without herself coming to the crisis; and then she could prolong the connection and achieve her orgasm and her crisis while he was merely a tool. (pp. 7–8)

Lawrence bluntly satirizes feminist and bohemian free love ideas which had been in circulation since before the Great War. His guiding notion is that civilization has tended to force apart mind and body, with the effect of turning sexual relationships into verbal meetings accompanied by mechanical sex, focused on the instrumental pleasure of two separate beings. In modern sex, each partner arrives at orgasm separately, remaining in rational control, rather than achieving mutual orgasm in an act of submission for the ego. Connie's first affair is with the bohemian Michaelis. They orgasm separately, and the affair is unsuccessful because inauthentic. With the gamekeeper Mellors Connie achieves mutual orgasm, because she is prepared to submit rather than remain in control. This relationship is depicted as authentic since the submission of the ego returns Connie to a more authentic state in which body and mind do not exist as opposing forces. This is a more 'primitive' state, perhaps, but Lawrence does not advocate a return to pre-civilization. Rather, he examines the ways in which an imagined unity of mind and body has become lost, and the ways in which it can be glimpsed or rediscovered in industrial modernity.

We may not wish to subscribe to any of Lawrence's own varying accounts of marriage and heterosexual relationship; indeed, several commentators have highlighted Lawrence's own problematic relationships with women, and concentrated on the sexism of his fictional ideology. Without wishing simply to exculpate him, it is illuminating to remind ourselves how he arrived at this kind of position. It is clear that Lawrence highlights the loss of nature in civilized society, and takes for granted the opposition between mind and matter, society and nature, which is the legacy of Romantic thought. In some respects, Lawrence's tendency to think in these terms recalls Langston Hughes's frustration at the tendency of whites to demand primitivism from black art, while African Americans sought to be assimilated to white bohemia in a culture which would leave behind supposedly primitive roots.

Despite the difference of context, Lawrence's own biographical trajectory is not dissimilar to that of people such as Langston Hughes, who in an attempt to develop himself beyond his provincial background became an artist and sought like-minded company among generally more privileged and sophisticated people who cast themselves in the same vein. The ideas of white liberal bohemia certainly appear progressive enough. They value the individual and free expression, and call for freedom in love away from the property-bound confinement of middle-class marriage. Despite this, these sects, with their ideology of art, also prove ultimately dissatisfying to the outsiders, such as Hughes and Lawrence, who join them. Yet art offers a promise of individuation, growth and self-expression which is a lifeline to anyone seeking freedom, especially to someone whose life-prospects seem limited because of his or her origin.

Lawrence's novels incorporate a varying amount of autobiographical material relating to his own attempt to develop beyond his environment. Perhaps his finest and most appreciated novel is still the highly autobiographical *Sons and Lovers* (1913), in which he draws a thinly veiled picture of himself as the aspiring artist Paul Morel, like Lawrence the son of a collier. The dominant theme of the work is Morel's relationship with women, his mother and girlfriends, Miriam Leivers and Clara Dawes. The tenet of Paul's troubled relationships with girls is a sense of something in himself which cannot be fully answered by any particular relationship – although Lawrence's candid emotional exploration indicates that the dominance of his relationship with his mother helps to make other relationships seem incomplete and unsatisfactory. Miriam, who wants to marry him, concludes that his mother is the obstacle: 'He had come back to his mother. Hers was the strongest tie in his life.'[10] Paul glosses this with a different emphasis: 'I don't think one person would ever monopolize me – be everything to me – I think never' (p. 265). Clara Dawes, who also must come to terms with the fact that she can never marry Paul, arrives at a slightly different conclusion: 'She knew she never fully had him: some part, big and vital in him, she had no hold over; nor did she ever try to get to it, or even to realize what it was' (p. 405).

The shift of emphasis in these three accounts of Paul's unavailability takes us from the simply Freudian (his relationship with his mother) to a broader concept of his dissatisfaction which is represented by the term 'vital'. *Lady Chatterley's Lover* repeatedly makes this contrast between the vital and non-vital, between the live and the dead, and indeed Lawrence uses these terms throughout his work. At times he draws on the idea of 'will' to represent this vitality, with reference to Friedrich Nietzsche's will to power. Lawrence eventually rejected what he saw as the overemphasis on mind inherent in Nietzsche's concept, but continued to use the term alongside the simpler notion of 'life' as an assertion of a principle of human becoming and growth which could not be contained by the mechanical world.

It would be useless to pretend that Lawrence's stance is anything like philosophical, since above all in his work he cherishes a subject-ive and intuitive freedom. Nevertheless, his work closely chimes with waxing and waning enthusiasms in his own time for the vitalism of Nietzsche, of Arthur Schopenhauer and of Henri Bergson, whose *Matter and Memory* (1896) attempted to theorize the body as a site of freedom of action in an otherwise mechanically determined world, and whose *Creative Evolution* (1907) attempted to account for evolution itself in terms of the unfolding of an interior life force he termed *élan vital*.

In his adoption of a loosely vitalist position, Lawrence was led to assign the terms 'live' and 'dead' to people and cultural phenomena, as we have already seen. On the one hand, vitalism gave him a means to account for his own restlessness, creativity and need to escape his environment. On the other, this mode of thinking mired him in a binarism which led to conclusions that look questionable even while the issue they attempt to tackle – the increasing confinement of human life in an increasingly rationalized and industrialized world – seems eminently valid.

Focus on the numerous ideological impasses in which Lawrence found himself tends to obscure what is important about his work. Lawrence in his life trod a remarkable path from the working class, via literary bohemia, into an astonishing self-exile and search for authentic being in Italy, Australia and finally New Mexico. His dissat-isfaction with the limits of the life offered him as a collier's son grew into a dissatisfaction with industrial modernity and modern Western thought in its entirety. The best moments in his work are reflected perhaps not in the numerous passages in which one theory or another of the importance of 'life' and the 'deadness' of others is asserted, but in the many subtle portrayals – especially in the earlier novels and stories – of moments of dissatisfaction in lives which seek fulfilment. It is Lawrence's own dissatisfaction which informs these moments, even where, as in *The Rainbow* (1915), it is the rural women who are the carriers of the movement from unreflective immersion in the cycle of daily life to something more:

> But the woman wanted another form of life than this, something that was not blood-intimacy. Her house faced out from the farm-buildings and fields [. . .]. Looking out, as she must, from the front of her house towards the activities of man in the world at large, whilst her husband

looked out to the back at sky and harvest and beast and land, she strained her eyes to see what man had done in fighting outwards toward knowledge [. . .]. She also wanted to know and be of the fighting host.[11]

Lawrence is the great writer of the English working class in the twentieth century because, at his best, he documents the confinement of individual lives, while asserting the spirit which wishes to escape that confinement and rejecting the contemporary alternatives, especially where, as in the case of sexual morality and jazz, modernity has failed to live up to his demanding ontology.

CHAPTER 8

Virginia Woolf: Art and Class

Virginia Woolf is now usually thought of as a feminist author. Yet the term 'feminist' has a number of meanings, and it is worth considering in what ways the word applies to Woolf. In both her own creative practice and her essays, she shows herself to be a keen advocate of women as writers and of a women's literary tradition. Her literary politics are certainly feminist. In terms of content, it is also clear that Woolf asks questions about women's art, the nature of female consciousness, and the appropriate means of literary presentation that must be developed to make the nature of a feminine consciousness visible. Yet she reveals herself as having a particular kind of feminist stance which is pessimistic about most of the forms of feminist politics which were available to her in her own time. As her relationship with Vita Sackville West, and the tribute to Vita's androgyny paid by Woolf's novel *Orlando* (1928), demonstrate, Woolf responded in some ways to the idea of sexual liberation which had been moving through the upper middle classes since before World War I. Nevertheless, we find little identification between Woolf and the feminist movement which existed at the time on a large scale. Before the war, feminism had almost exclusively taken the form of suffragism and an idea of the New Woman sponsored by the upper middle class. After the war, the notion of equality between the sexes was superseded among the majority of left-wing women by the notion of equality between classes – a notion of the struggle for equality for all advocated by the increasingly popular labour and communist movements.

In this respect, we find that Woolf is quite as distant from the aspirations of the working-class movement as was T. S. Eliot, even if

Virginia Woolf: Art and Class

Eliot's royalism contrasts with Woolf's general scepticism towards the institutions of (post-)imperial British society. While remaining critical of the present society, Woolf appears to find little cause for optimism in the theories of social progress which were available to her. In her anti-war tract *Three Guineas* (1938), she argued that her class, which she referred to as the 'daughters of educated men', was politically the weakest in the state:

> If the working women of the country were to say: 'If you go to war, we will refuse to make munitions or to help in the production of goods,' the difficulty of war-making would be seriously increased. But if all the daughters of educated men were to down tools to-morrow, nothing essential either to the life or to the war-making of the community would be embarrassed. Our class is the weakest of all the classes in the state. We have no weapon with which to enforce our will.[1]

Although Woolf is discussing the coming world war, her point of reference is the previous one. In particular, she mentions the status of working-class women and contrasts what she perceives as their potential political leverage, as a class of workers, with her own lack of leverage, as one of the 'daughters of educated men'. 'Educated men' are those who have passed through the principal educational structure of the ruling classes, but whose influence stems from their education rather than from their economic power. As Woolf notes, these men still have some sort of influence in the politics of the state because of their education and connections, although, as I have pointed out in chapter 5, the period after World War I represents a time of crisis for the educated class, who believed that their influence was diminishing proportionally as the power of trade unions grew. The 'daughters of educated men', in Woolf's account, are doubly disadvantaged, as they do not even have the education of their fathers, since until recently women had been excluded from full access to the universities and the professions.

What we need to note in this is that the modern category of feminism, which is frequently applied to Woolf, does not properly fit her own explicit analysis of her situation. Modern feminism, as it has developed since the 1960s, has loosely borrowed from Marxism the insight that workers of the world have common interests, stemming from the fact that they are all workers, regardless of ethnicity or nationality. Feminism advanced the claim that women of the world could be united as a class, since regardless of differences of ethnicity and of social class, they had common interests arising from the fact that all were women. The strength of this position, for those who adopt it, is obvious, since it allows any woman who declares that she is speaking 'as a woman' to make claims for all women. What we should note, here, is that Woolf very carefully disavows this stance. She does not claim to speak for all women, although she does assume that working women and the daughters of educated men *might* adopt a similar anti-war stance. Like the feminists of the 1970s, Woolf borrows from Marxism the view that society is divided into classes which have different interests, and proposes further subdivisions within the recognized classes, based on gender.

It is not my intention here to debate the relative merits of these positions, rather to point out that Woolf does not argue for the universal interests of women, but is instead focused on her own class and its functioning. Even though she asserts the right of women to write in *A Room of One's Own* (1929), she is asserting a kind of professional right rather than a universal one. At a time of dramatic class distinctions at the level of money and manners it may be no surprise that Woolf did not defend any universal notion of womanhood, but it is worth reminding ourselves that her stance was formulated in conscious resistance to those who did.

By way of contrast, I would like to examine a text by an entirely unknown woman writer, part of which deals with World War I and its aftermath in the context of the lives of working women. Maggie Newbery's *Picking Up Threads: Reminiscences of a Bradford Mill Girl* (1980),[2] written in the 1970s, is the story of a woman born in 1901. The style is plain and required revision by a second hand, and its composition invited the mild mockery of relatives who had been led to believe that poor people should not write their 'memoirs' – that is, document their lives. It is a valuable document of life in the major mill city of Bradford, and all the more revealing for the author's political and literary naivety. As was common at that time, Maggie started working at the age of 12 on a half-time basis while continuing at school. This meant a working day of up to 6 hours, in the context of a full adult working week of 55 hours plus compulsory overtime when required by the employer: the 1870 Education Act notoriously allowed for 'half-time' schooling of 10 hours a week if a child was working. Of three meals in a day, two would probably consist of bread and jam and tea. Maggie's account of her childhood juxtaposes passages describing brutal conditions at work with accounts of children's games which she would play in the evening. There is a stark contrast between the exploitation of these young girls, who would usually be set to full-time work from their fourteenth birthdays, and the received notion of employment as an 'opportunity' for women. Mill work was regarded as one step up in status and desirability from domestic service – the lowest possible station as far as these mill girls were concerned – and a girl with a well-paid husband could hope to leave the labour market altogether. Maggie's family were Methodists, and their self-discipline kept them comparatively buoyant, while others sank further into poverty and succumbed to disease. At 13 years of age Maggie was quite aware of suffragism:

> We did pay attention to the Suffragette Movement; we found something funny in the idea of votes for women. They had a meeting room in what used to be a shop on Manningham Lane. Wherever we were passing, if there were signs of activity there, we would walk very quietly up to the door, open it quickly and all yell together, 'votes for women' in a derisory way. It was one way of letting off steam. (p. 54)

Maggie does not draw any conclusions from this recollection, although we should recall both that the suffrage movement did not argue for universal suffrage, and that it was the subject of continuous press vilification.

Now working full time, Maggie spent World War I in the mill, her labour very much in demand for the war effort, although she still hoped to leave and become a teacher, trying and failing to be accepted at night school. When the war ended, and confirming more recent accounts which have failed to find any significant increase in female employment after the war, mills closed or moved back to continental Europe, and Maggie was made redundant. In the 1920s she was employed periodically as a sewing-machine home representative and a nurse (herself virtually a prisoner of the institution, Menston Asylum), finally discovering her metier as a swimming instructor.

Those who believe that women's political understanding awaited the publication of *A Room of One's Own* in 1929 (dubbed by one commentator the 'feminist Bible') need only go back to the example of Eleanor Marx (1855–98) to discover a whole trajectory of women's politics in the labour movement which ruling-class authors and activists such as Suffragists and Fabians largely despised and ignored. This is not the place for an exposition of the political career of Eleanor Marx – Yvonne Kapp's 1972 biography remains a landmark – but Maggie Newbery, who lacked education and any political ambition, offers an example of how far the political aspirations of even the least enabled women advanced as a consequence of their historical experience. So in 1917 the Russian Revolution was well known to English workers, and Maggie Newbery, with no political axe to grind, writes simply as follows:

> At this time in the mill we heard a lot about Russian workers uniting to overthrow their Government, and some of us thought it was quite a good idea. I think the workers all over the world were waking up to the injustices done to the working class. We mill workers had the evidence before our eyes of the mansions the mill workers lived in, while we were always on the poverty line and one week from the workhouse, as the older ones put it. The workers were beginning to real-ize that the only way to better their lot was to unite. The miner's slogan of eight hours' work, eight hours' play, eight hours' sleep and eight bob [shillings] a day was taken up by the dockers, and we in the mills began to think we ought to have a little more of this world's goods. (p. 82)

Maggie was 16 at the time and the war was still far from over. After the war, she became involved in the Guild of Youth and the Labour Party:

> Most of the young people in the Guild were very serious thinkers and were determined to get a better deal for the workers of this country, so a lot of our time was taken up with work for the Labour Party. It was at this time too that the Labour Party took St George's Hall for their speakers every Saturday night and I had the pleasure of hearing some of the finest politicians of the day speak in that hall to capacity crowds. After the meeting we would sell the labour paper to the crowds as they left. (p. 94)

Family disagreements ensued:

> My father would argue with me sometimes about the Labour Party. He remained a staunch Conservative. Don't you see, he would say, the Conservatives are educated and you must have educated men at the top. To which I would reply, and what's wrong with the Labour people being educated? We know we are ignorant and if a university education is good for the monied class, then it is good for the worker and that's just what we want: the chance to go on, and go to the university and learn to express ourselves, so that we can have a voice in the government. (p. 94)

This was before the election of the first Labour government of Ramsay MacDonald. Maggie Newbery's account reminds us that universal access to education at all levels was an established objective of the rank-and-file labour movement, and tells us something about the common social experiences which generated such demands. One commentator notes 'the prescience of Woolf's ideas and her capacity to anticipate the concerns of feminism in the future',[3] a remark which reflects the tenor of much of the apologetics surrounding her work. But Woolf also had an uncanny ability to ignore the demands of women which had already been formulated and were widely disseminated, as Maggie Newbery testifies, and it is no disservice to the understanding of Woolf's work to set her own claims against popular aspirations: I doubt whether she herself could have believed that so much of women's politics and history would be so casually eclipsed as it has been by such highly partial commentaries.

I want to use this reflection on Woolf's political stance to shift the emphasis in our reading of her away from a simplistic model of Woolf-as-feminist, in order to reflect on what she has in common with other modernists – her exploration of art as a stance within existing social reality. We have already said that pre-war art in general was a reaction against what was perceived as the stifling nature of bourgeois society. World War I and the Russian Revolution threw up the organized working class as a more robust opponent of bourgeois society and values than was art, and independent intellectuals in the middle ground found themselves searching to redefine their role. In this respect, Woolf has much in common with figures such as Wyndham Lewis and Eliot, in that she asks questions about the social role of art, the position of the independent thinker (of which the 'daughters of educated men' are the female wing), and the legitimacy or otherwise of regarding art as something that might transcend society. She asks too the cognate question of whether the artist can transcend society and adopt a role independent of the ruling class and its nemesis the proletariat.

So the question of art, as it often appears in Woolf's works, should not be construed simply as a question about women's opportunities in the world of art, although certainly this is a theme. We can see this theme as it appears, famously, in *To the Lighthouse*, in the character of Lily Briscoe, who avoids marriage and attempts art in defiance of social convention. She is discouraged by Mr Tansley, whose announcement that 'women can't paint, women can't write' haunts her as she bends over her easel.[4] In a straightforward manner, Woolf signals the theme of *A Room of One's Own*, by dramatizing the social discouragement that she believes attends the cultural efforts of all women. This theme will be uppermost in the mind of most readers, who will perhaps be less aware that there are further questions lurking here. What is art and why should it be practised? What does art have to do with femininity? What does class have to do with art?

Art, women and class are on full view in *To the Lighthouse*. Woolf depicts the family of an 'educated man' at a holiday home located (implausibly) in the Hebrides, based in fact on the holidays of her own family in St Ives, Cornwall. The figure of Mr Ramsay is based in part on Woolf's father, Sir Leslie Stephen, and Mrs Ramsay on her mother Julia. In developing a picture of her family, Woolf is particularly influenced by the ideas and methods of modern art. This is signalled clearly by the figure of Lily Briscoe, one of a number of guests at the house, who is seen in the process of making a painting of Mrs Ramsay according to principles which are clearly those of post-Impressionism. Her painting is not a direct representation, but a formal rearrangement of the elements she has in front of her into a pattern of 'mass', 'line' and 'colour' (p. 22). As Lily reflects to herself, her portrait of Mrs Ramsay seated at the window of the house expresses not the idea 'I'm in love with you' but the idea 'I'm in love with this all' (p. 24). Lily's painting is an exercise in formal organization, as she reveals to an onlooker, Mr Bankes:

What did she wish to indicate by the triangular purple shape, 'just there?' he asked.

It was Mrs. Ramsay reading to James, she said. She knew his objection – that no one could tell it for a human shape. But she had made no attempt at likeness, she said. For what reason had she introduced them then? he asked. Why indeed? – except that if there, in that corner, it was bright, here, in this one, she felt the need of darkness. (pp. 58–9)

Lily's art plainly reflects the stance of the post-Impressionism of Picasso and Braque, which was introduced to Londoners by Woolf's friend Roger Fry, who explained the impact of modern art on the 'ordinary man, whose vision is limited to the mere recognition of objects with a view to the uses of everyday life'. Against this expectation that art be representational, the modern movement asserted 'the re-establishment of purely aesthetic criteria in place of the criterion of conformity to appearance' and 'the rediscovery of the principles of formal design and harmony'.[5]

In 'An Essay on the Aesthetic', Roger Fry insists that art create its emotional effect purely through the arrangement of line, mass, space, light and shade, and colour. He rejects the argument of Tolstoy in *What is Art?* that art must be judged purely in terms of its moral effect, its 'reaction upon actual life'.[6] This idea is reflected in Lily's approach to her subject, as Mr Bankes notes: 'Mother and child then – objects of universal veneration, and in this case the mother was famous for her beauty – might be reduced, he pondered, to a purple shadow without irreverence' (p. 59). Woolf introduces this discussion of Lily's painting in *To the Lighthouse* not simply to indicate that Lily's ideas are in advance of the male-dominated milieu in which she finds herself, but in order to suggest the analogy between the post-Impressionist view of art and the questions that she has had to resolve in order to develop the medium in which she is now herself working.

The analogy between one art and another can never be simple. It is likely to emerge as a broad parallel in which the difference of medium, and the different historical trajectories of that medium, ensure that the analogy consists more of difference than of similarity. Nevertheless, it is clear that Woolf has asked herself what it might mean to bring the qualities of recent developments in the visual arts into the field of the novel, with the important qualifier that what emerges must still clearly *be* a novel. She had a clear example and model in front of her – *Ulysses*, which, as an enormous challenge to the autonomy of her own art, she both disavowed and imitated. *Ulysses*, which divides its narrative into one-hour segments, was very clearly the model for *Mrs Dalloway*, which was originally called *The Hours*, and adopted the third person centre-of-consciousness narrative which is the hallmark of large sections of James Joyce's work. Woolf discerned that Joyce's topic – empire – and his methodology, which concerned the nature of choice and judgement in the context of environmental determination, were fundamentally close to her own concerns.

In *Ulysses*, Joyce had introduced prose styles of increasing complexity and difficulty as the work progressed. The result was a massive work which posed a huge challenge to contemporary readers. It is likely that Woolf felt that *Ulysses* went beyond the scope of the novel, and that she decided to harness exactly those features of it which remained novelistic and could still be accessed by the 'common reader'. So her narratives are shorter in length but not necessarily narrower in scope than that of Joyce.

In using the third person centre-of-consciousness technique, Woolf constructed a novelistic surface which had certain affinities with the ideas of modern art espoused by Fry and others. He had emphasized that the medium of art should not be representational, and should not be fashioned with a view to its impact on the actual, moral world. Woolf's technique is sometimes referred to loosely as 'stream of consciousness'. This term documents the fact that her style is designed to narrate the content of consciousnesses, but is a little approximate. I have preferred the term 'third person centre of consciousness' for its greater precision. In general, the narrative of *Mrs Dalloway* and *To the Lighthouse* presents the consciousness of various characters in an idiom which sometimes is borrowed from the minds and voices of the characters, and at other times is cast in a narrative voice which is independent of the character(s) even while it narrates according to their thoughts or knowledge. This means that there is a still an authorial narrative voice present. Moreover, this is a narrator who in terms of English idiom entirely shares the milieu of the upper middle-class characters who are the principal topic of the narrative.

Woolf's model is as much Jane Austen as anything said by Roger Fry, as her motivating notion appears to be that prose narrative style *cannot* simply adopt the formal objectivity and moral disinterestedness of painting, since words are not merely sensory and since the language of society which the author uses is automatically one of judgement. However, Woolf wants to make this narrative idiom formally independent to a degree, since the judgements of individual characters become a key element in the medium, and these judgements are referred to the minds of individual characters and are therefore *immanent* in the society – that is, the judgements about characters do not come from an outside view which transcends the society which is being depicted, but lie within that society and within the range of its possible points of view. At times we find that we cannot distinguish the opinion of a character from that of the author. This is because Woolf does not create a narrator who lies outside or beyond judgement, but accepts that as narrator she is part of that society and of its possible ranges of judgement. So, the fact that Mrs Ramsay is viewed positively by certain characters in *To the Lighthouse* becomes mixed in the reader's mind with the possibility that the author also views Mrs Ramsay positively.

The important qualification here is that Woolf has also learned from Joyce that an idiom can be objective, and that a novel deals in social judgements which can have a scientific and political inflection as well as a more straightforwardly personal and immanent one. Joyce depicted a society which he loved, but which he was also able to see in terms of environmental conditioning, as did naturalist novelists such as Honoré de Balzac. Woolf was suited by the complex perspective allowed by this standpoint and the narrative style which accompanied it. This enables her to construct narratives which can sympathize with their principals and, at the same time, depict the nature of their environmental conditioning. Specifically, Woolf can sympathize with her female protagonists while still being careful to show how they are complicit with the British imperialism which is their whole *raison d'être*. The analogy with painting has led her to ask whether a narrative can be constructed which might be as object-like as a post-Impressionist painting, in that the field of judgements which gives a novel (as opposed to a painting) its meaning can itself be rendered somehow objective, and somehow beautiful.

Of course, this is a difficult task, but if we recognize that Woolf is assembling a novel which is art, in the same way as Fry or Lily Briscoe think of a painting as being art, then we avoid being too simplistic in our moral assessments of Woolf's characters. However, she does not withdraw from her narrative completely. On the contrary, she is as much of a mediating presence as Austen in her novels, and it is her own voice – and her own class idiom – which create the ether through which the characters collectively move. This could be seen as a limitation on Woolf's art, but it is more productive to see it as a recognition of her own limits (in terms of her range of sympathies and experience) and of the limits of fictional art as such. Fiction is essentially a moral medium in terms both of its subjects and of its readership, and this moral vocation can only be transcended in a limited way.

For example, take this passage, in which Mrs Ramsay addresses Mr Tansley at the dinner she has organized:

> 'How you must detest dining in this bear garden,' she said, making use, as she did when she was distracted, of her social manner. [. . .] Mr. Tansley, who had no knowledge of this language, even spoken thus in words of one syllable, at once suspected its insincerity. They did talk nonsense, he thought, the Ramsays; and he pounced on this fresh instance with joy, making a note which, one of these days, he would read aloud, to one or two friends. There, in a society in which one could say what one liked he would sarcastically describe 'staying with the Ramsays' and what nonsense they talked. (p. 98)

Throughout the section from which this quotation is taken, the narrative passes from one character to another, exploring their conversation and the mental activity which accompanies it. In this passage, the narrative passes from Mrs Ramsay to Mr Tansley. Mrs Ramsay is in many ways the central figure of *To the Lighthouse*. Woolf has asked herself in this novel something about how she must see her own mother. Yet Mrs Ramsay is not altogether a portrait. For Woolf has also asked the question in the narrative about how we know another person at all. Opinions and impressions may vary over time, even from moment to moment, and the narrative structure is designed to show this process at work. However, in showing points of view which are those of individual characters and can therefore be said to be immanent to the narrative, the narrative does not renounce an authorial viewpoint which is independent of the characters.

So in the above passage we find a claim about Mrs Ramsay which does not evidently belong to any other character, but to an authorial voice: 'making use, as she did when she was distracted, of her social manner'. This phrase is *explanatory*. The authorial voice is forcibly present as the medium of the reader's understanding. We must be told that Mrs Ramsay is using her 'social manner' in order to be able properly to evaluate Mr Tansley's response. Put simply, the authorial voice, or the mediating authorial presence, is broadly guiding us into sympathy with Mrs Ramsay, and against the intellectual resentment of the outsider Tansley. He receives the most negative portrayal of any character in the novel, coming to stand in the novel's scale of values for the worst aspects of male culture. So here, when his response to Mrs Ramsay is mapped out, the narrative voice moves seamlessly from description of his thoughts to speculation about his future actions, speculation which *may* be part of his thoughts, or may be an authorial extension of them. This is left ambiguous. However, the future scenario of Tansley mocking the life of the Ramsays with a few carefully chosen intellectual companions is presented more in the spirit of satire on the college man than as a naturalistic portrayal of Tansley's thought.

The controlling presence of an author in this narrative voice is important to the provision of a moral centre of gravity. The author is not a powerful presence making *ex cathedra* pronouncements on her characters, but an implicit presence set back in the medium of the narrative itself, much as the colour blue is the defining ground and binding medium of the works of Picasso's blue period.

However, it is the reassuring presence of this authorial medium, combined with a set of assumptions about the nature of Woolf's 'feminism', that has also led to misunderstanding of the goals of her novels. In the above passage, we saw how the authorial medium steered the reader to appreciate Mrs Ramsay's virtue and reject Mr Tansley's disdain for her 'social manner'. It is not only a matter of judgement of character, but a matter of social judgement too, that against a background of diminishing respect for the upper classes, Woolf chooses to mount a qualified defence of the 'social manner' of those classes and imply its importance as a type of binding social medium even if its class nature and restricted sincerity are only too evident. In fact, in both *To the Lighthouse* and *Mrs Dalloway*, Woolf examines the figure of the mother in a wealthy family as a hostess, and depicts the role of the hostess in her ability to bind together otherwise isolated consciousnesses. The hostess is thus a kind of artist of the moment, and the implied idea of an art of the moment is a reflection on the nature of art, which, it can be inferred, should be more momentary and relational, less monumental and transcendental. The feminine art of the hostess is in some ways contrasted with the masculine art of the artist.

Although Woolf's fiction celebrates certain aspects of the woman-as-hostess, we should not conclude that, in some straightforward fashion, Woolf is taking the side of these wealthy women against their detractors, and against their husbands. This would be to ignore another field of values altogether: that of the naturalist novelist who is depicting the dynamics of social reality with an objective as well as an involved eye. For while the authorial voice of *To the Lighthouse* seems to steer us into the love of Mrs Ramsay which is shared by those around her, Woolf is also showing how family and love relationships work to perpetuate the economic and social system. In this respect, not only Mrs Dalloway but even the revered Mrs Ramsay are set before us as people who are complicit with the whole project of empire to which Woolf herself is unsympathetic. She has asked a deep-seated moral question of herself and of those who would read novels in identification with her own social group: how is it possible to respect and love one's own friends, family and past, if it is clear from a politicized perspective that every aspect of life in that class (including the gendered division of labour which creates roles for 'mother' and 'father') is conditioned by the goal of empire and of self-reproduction of the class? Or if the right to reject one's past and fight against it has been eclipsed by the fact that others (in *To the Lighthouse*, Mr Tansley, in *Mrs Dalloway*, the resentful and poor Miss Kilman) hate and reject your class with more vehemence than one could ever manage oneself? I have used Woolf's own class-laden 'one' not merely as a device to structure this sentence but to try more effectively to paraphrase the innermost thought of these narratives which the medium allows the author to shape.

Because in so many ways we are made to feel that we know where the author is coming from, it is possible to overlook that Woolf proposes a critique of her whole class, and that her presentation of female characters looks at the nature of their complicity in the perpetuation of class rule and the empire over which the British upper classes preside. This theme is announced on the first page of *To the Lighthouse*, which presents the scene of Mrs Ramsay overseeing her son, James, at play. James is seen cutting images out of a shopping catalogue – Woolf makes it the catalogue of the Army and Navy Store in order quietly to point up that the nature of the imperial British state is always, irreducibly, her topic. That James is cutting out is also a symbolic fact, since in the context of Woolf's fiction to cut something out is an operation of mind or culture which interrupts the flow of life as continuous duration. Cutting out often has masculine associations in Woolf's work, but art too is a form of cutting out since it frames an image of the momentary texture of reality and gives the moment a kind of stasis and permanence. However, cutting is not wholly masculine, as can be seen in *Mrs Dalloway*, where, although the mid-life crisis of Peter Walsh is symbolically embodied in the fact that he plays with his pocket knife, it is Clarissa Dalloway herself who is identified as a blade, who indeed has 'cut out' her servant's work on the first page of the narrative.

Although the cutting here is certainly an emblem of the masculinity of James's mind, it is his mother's attitude which we should note:

His mother, watching him guide his scissors neatly round the refriger-ator, imagined him all red and ermine on the Bench or directing a stern and momentous enterprise in some crisis of public affairs. (p. 7)

Mrs Ramsay is not really conscious of her role in building this stern masculine character. She unwittingly encourages in James the Promethean qualities of the adventurer or soldier which are needed in the men who will run the empire:

When she read just now to James, 'and there were numbers of soldiers with kettle-drums and trumpets', and his eyes darkened, she thought, why should they grow up and lose all that? He was the most gifted, the most sensitive of her children. (p. 65)

One point here is the authorial irony, which makes Mrs Ramsay see the material she feeds James as childish, unconnected with the adult world, and the implied authorial position which asserts that the glory of war is indeed a fundamental value of male adult life in the context of empire. The notion that James is 'gifted and sensitive' has to be read against Woolf's earlier novel, *Jacob's Room*, which deals with another gifted and sensitive young man, whose very sensitivity is shown to be part of his preparation for war. In this, she is correcting the easily adopted view that the educated elite of Cambridge young men might reject war and empire. On the contrary, her work suggests, these men in all their sensitivity and complexity are the cornerstones of empire, its most idealistic protagonists.

Once we acknowledge that Woolf is looking at the issue of how family life forms the adults of the future, we may well wish to reject the customary reading of the opening incident of *To the Lighthouse*. This commonly adopted interpretation criticizes the father, Mr Ramsay, for saying that weather will not permit an expedition to the light-house, and praises Mrs Ramsay for saying that the expedition might be possible. What we might now wish to say is that Mrs Ramsay unwittingly encourages James in the fantasy of overcoming imposs-ible obstacles which is a key quality required in the young men who will take over the project of empire. She encourages dream and fantasy, believing that children should be encouraged to fantasize and not be discouraged by the intrusion of reality. Thus all men in this rank of society are encouraged to think of themselves as leading impossible expeditions such as that of Robert Falcon Scott, whose expedition to the South Pole of 1911–12 famously ended with his death on the return journey. Woolf shows that this ideology of pathos-laden death and self-sacrifice in the attempt to attain remote goals is a central plank of the British imperial ideology, influencing not merely men of action but thinkers such as Mr Ramsay, who sees his impossible quest for philosophical finality as if it were an expedi-tion, like Scott's journey to the pole:

He dug his heels in at Q. Q he was sure of. Q he could demonstrate. If Q then is Q – R – [. . .]

Qualities that would have saved a ship's company exposed on a broiling sea with six biscuits and a flask of water – endurance and justice, foresight, devotion, skill, came to his help. R then is – what is R? [. . .]

In that flash of darkness he heard people saying – he was a failure – that R was beyond him. He would never reach R. On to R, once more. R –

Qualities that in a desolate expedition across the icy solitudes of the Polar region would have made him the leader, the guide, the counsellor, whose temper, neither sanguine nor despondent, surveys with

equanimity what is to be and faces it, came to his help again. R – .
(pp. 39–40)

Here the analysis comes full circle, and we see how Woolf has established the novel as a medium in which, on the one hand, judgements
are made and circulated, and, on the other, a process of objectification
is at work which sees each side of the gender division in the upper-
class Edwardian family as part of the imperial process itself – a process
which, as Woolf depicts it, seems strangely in difficulty when it comes
to analysing and correcting itself.

The final question facing Woolf is, then, this: if male intellectual
culture in general is compromised by an obsession with transcendence that is merely a cerebral version of ruling-class male imperial
ideology, can a female art provide an alternative? Art, like thought,
defies immersion in the moment and in the seamless fabric of
experience and of the everyday. Yet, like thought, art offers a type of
transcendence and semi-permanence which is fashioned from experience and from the present moment. *To the Lighthouse*, in its examination
of the art of Lily Briscoe, tentatively suggests the importance of art in
transfiguring the moment, but in melancholy fashion leaves us with a
vision of Lily's painting confined to a future attic, not as sitting in a
gallery, informing the future about the past that once was. A pessimistic
conclusion: yet Woolf could surely have been more assertive about
art, since her own style is designed to be this very form of art which
will both involve itself in the individual moment and restore the
complex texture of intersecting experiences, into something that
is sufficiently fixed and stable to present itself as an object for knowledge and thought.

CHAPTER 9

The Modernity of Adorno and Benjamin

As we have already established, the high modernist authors were not intent simply on producing an art which in its forms and languages was the *reflection* of technological and social changes, but one which *reflected on* a changing society and gave an account of it. Ezra Pound, T. S. Eliot, Wyndham Lewis and D. H. Lawrence react notably against mass society and technical modernity, linking themselves loosely to Italian Fascism (Pound) or the French Catholic reaction (Eliot and Lewis), or asserting the vitality and independence of the artist in a philosophy loosely derived from Arthur Schopenhauer and Friedrich Nietzsche (Lewis and Lawrence). The political and social tendency of James Joyce's work is not agreed among commentators, but I have argued here that there is a case for seeing him as a naturalist documenting the elusive relationship between mind and body in imperial, gendered society. Virginia Woolf is more evidently systematic in her pessimist-feminist analysis of the relationship between individual, family and society in the context of the ruling groups within late British imperialism.

Each of these writers develops, across his or her work, elaborate models of individuality and consciousness as products of sexualized, gendered bodies in collision with alien and frequently coercive external forces. Concerns of this type are also evidenced in the work of writers such as Mina Loy, whose oeuvres are smaller and therefore less global or systematic in their implications. Why then, if modernist literature is so evidently socially and theoretically self-aware, do so many of its commentators look beyond that literature, and beyond English-language culture, in an attempt to reflect both on modernist art and on the social modernity which produced it?

There are two main reasons. Despite its apparent social-theoretical awareness, many readers have found modernism either to be inadequate in its thinking, or at the very least insufficiently explicit, in this regard. Moreover, the complex textual operations of many modernist texts are never adequately explained by the writers (or by their contemporaries) and call for additional commentary, both in order that they might be better appreciated, and in order that the implications of these works as textual artefacts might be properly articulated.

In respect of issues concerning textuality, critics have invested heavily in deconstruction and the work of Jacques Derrida, which we examine in the following chapter. In respect of the cultural-theoretical analysis of modernity, they have turned to the work of Theodor Adorno, Walter Benjamin, and a selection of their contemporaries such as Georg Lukács.

Adorno and Benjamin are attractive figures for two reasons. One is their immersion in a theoretically self-conscious form of discourse – in Adorno's case, informed by the tradition of Hegelian Marxism. The other is their commitment to analysing the social situation of various fields of art, including mass entertainment. Although Lewis is present in the canon of Anglo-American modernism as a parallel figure to Adorno and Benjamin in terms of the range and ambition of his cultural criticism, it is to these left-wing figures in the German tradition that most commentators turn to supplement their sense of literary modernism with a diet of cultural modernist theory.

The juxtaposition of left-wing German theory with Anglo-American literature does not yield any tidy examples of the one being used to illuminate the other. Indeed, there are important asymmetries which in themselves constitute the reason that Adorno and Benjamin are read *alongside* literary modernism rather than as a commentary on it. While high modernism has World War I as its centre of gravity, these analysts of modernity are rooted essentially in the 1930s, and the questions they ask have in the background a key historical event: the failure of the Russian Revolution to reproduce itself in Germany, and the ascendancy of Nazism.

Karl Marx had argued that communist revolution spearheaded by the working class (or proletariat) was inevitable in advanced industrial nations. It was in the rational self-interest of that class to create such a revolution and alter what Marx called the 'relations of production' (that is, the existing class structure) to keep pace with the 'means of production' (that is, the various technologies used within the society to produce necessary goods). If it was logical for the proletariat to take control of the wealth of society for the greater good, what prevented them from doing so once capitalism reached a sufficiently advanced point? Early in his career, in works such as *The German Ideology* (1845), Marx argued that people were led to mis-recognize reality by false ideas which were put into circulation. He referred to these false sets of ideas as 'ideology' and claimed that the dominant ideas of a time were those of the ruling class, ideas which justified the continuation of class society and masked the reasons for overturning existing social relations. In addition to the forces controlled by the state, such as the army and the police, it was ideas – ideology – which prevented people from understanding the real, material nature of society. The reality of production and social organization was held to be 'material', while ideas inhabited a ghostly unreality which reflected the real only in a distorted manner. These ideas were perpetuated by institutions which specialized in the dissemination of thinking, cultural institutions such as the church and schools.

Marx's theory of ideology is often discussed as if it were a constant feature of his thinking. This is questionable. He never explicitly renounces the theory; however, he ceases to mention it throughout the major late stage of his theoretical work which included *Grundrisse* (1857–8) and the three volumes of *Capital* (of which volume 1 was published in 1867). I believe that Marx lost interest in the theory of ideology because it was undialectical, by which I mean that it created an opposition between reality and the mask of ideas which left the material and the ideal independent of each other. The theory of ideology did not suggest a continuous reality, but one in which the material relations of society and the ideas held in the heads of individuals belonged to two separate realms. These two realms were discontinuous, and Marx as a dialectical thinker – as a thinker who sought to establish relationship and continuity – could not accept this discontinuity. What I have just said is necessarily speculative, since Marx never actually renounces the theory of ideology; however, it helps to explain why he develops a *second* theory to account for the inability of people to recognize the real nature of the society that they live in. This was the theory of the *commodity* as it is set out in the first book of *Capital*. The theory argued that people were misled about the nature of the social reality they occupied not by ideas, but by their relationship to things, specifically, to the manufactured things – food, clothes and so on – which made daily life possible. The nature of the commodity was such that it presented an *appearance* which masked reality. The *reality* behind the commodity was the whole network or structure of social and economic relationships which, for example, put the coat in the shop for someone to buy. Moreover, the *reality* of the commodity was that it was a simple object designed for *use*. However, the *appearance* which the commodity presented disguised both of these realities, since the commodity involved the exchange of money, an act which Marx held masked the reality of labour which had produced the commodity, as well as replacing its *use-value* with a fetishized *exchange-value* – that is to say, things appeared not as 'real' things but as objects of exchange. Thus the commodity itself disguised or mystified real social relations which were visible not as the relationship between people but as the cash relationship between things.

Marx, then, is trying to formulate a theory concerning why people in general, and the proletariat in particular, mis-recognize social reality, in order to explain what might prevent the proletariat from organizing a communist revolution. His *first* answer to this question is the theory of ideology, the claim that people are influenced by false *ideas* about society circulated by the ruling class and its institutions. His *second* answer to this question is the theory of the commodity, the claim that social reality is disguised by the material *objects* which confront people in everyday life.

Marx developed his theories in the second half of the nineteenth century; by the 1930s historical events had made the question of revolutionary consciousness much more pressing. The year 1917 had witnessed the Russian Revolution, led by Vladimir Lenin and the Bolshevik party. The fact that the revolution happened at all surprised communist theorists, who, following Marx, predicted that revolution would occur in the most industrially advanced nations. Russia had a predominantly agricultural economy and only a small industrial sector. The real confirmation of the validity of Marxist theory would come only if a comparable revolution occurred in Germany. With the defeat of Germany in World War I, German Marxists and socialists attempted to emulate the Russian Revolution, but despite temporary successes, especially in Berlin and Bavaria, a German workers' state did not materialize. Instead, a weak democratic state was created which was eventually usurped by Adolf Hitler's Nazis.

Left-wing thinkers in Germany in the 1930s asked how the German workers could be won away from socialism and seduced by Nazism. In this context, Marx's theories of false consciousness began to be revisited. Among practising political agitators, influenced by Lenin, the theory of the politicization of consciousness had revolved around the Communist Party acting as the vanguard of the working class, educating the workers both in theory and in practice. This was an entirely practical theory of political education and the raising of class consciousness. Activists did not require a highly elaborated theory of consciousness. However, intellectuals such as Lukács, Benjamin and Adorno saw that Marx lacked a developed theory of culture or of consciousness, and determined to develop this element of his work. The basic assumptions of each of these thinkers differed. Lukács was a revolutionary increasingly aligned with the Communist Party. Adorno had no such connection and was basically pessimistic about the prospect of social revolution, since capitalism so adeptly influences people at an unconscious level. Benjamin was both a utopian optimist and a natural pessimist, an individualistic speculator who lacked the immersion in the work of G. W. F. Hegel and Marx which conditioned the thinking of Lukács and Adorno.

Lukács is important not as an advocate of modernism in the arts – he denounced it – but as the figure who did most to introduce Hegelian Marxism into the process of theorizing art and artistic production. A key element in Lukács's Hegelian Marxist thinking is the opposition between the general and the particular. This opposition recurs in the thought of Adorno and of Benjamin in different ways. The importance of this opposition in Lukács's thinking depends in the first instance on Hegel, whose *Phenomenology of Spirit* (1807) rested on the logical distinction between immediate fact (appearance or particularity) and mediated knowledge (universality). Hegel described the evolution of human knowledge as a progression in which the apparent certainty of an 'immediate' fact or idea was realized to be a mere appearance, not with the result that the immediate particular should be seen as 'false', but that it must be placed in a higher and more complete framework of knowledge. So human knowledge moved constantly from the particular to the universal, from isolated pieces of knowledge to a grasp of the total process of life in the world. It was Hegel's claim that the modern state of humanity constituted a kind of 'absolute knowledge', in which reason had grasped the nature of the world and humankind's place within it. This was not a mystical idea, but a rational one, based on the assumption that the world and human existence within it could be grasped by reason.

Lukács, who realized that Hegel had continuing importance for Marx, saw that Marx's notion of the commodity rested on a similar distinction between the particular and the universal. In Marx's scheme, the commodity was a particular, a false appearance, which tended to prevent the mind from grasping the totality of social relationships which lay behind the commodity and set the pattern of its production and consumption. It is the job of *Capital* to analyse and present this totality, the true picture of how reality works, behind the false appearance of the commodity. Lukács, immersed in the history of the novel, formulated the parallel notion that literature must reveal the totality of the network of social relationships in order to demystify the reality of capitalism.

This led Lukács to assert the validity of the classic realist novel – the bourgeois novel of nineteenth-century capitalism – against the claims of the modernism of his own time. This might seem remarkable, given our emphasis in the present text on the social and political focus of modernism. The modernism to which Lukács referred in the context of the culture of Germany and other continental European countries was, however, different in nature to the Anglophone modernism we have so far examined. In his 1938 exchange with Ernst Bloch, who defended the avant-garde, Lukács makes reference to Expressionism and Surrealism, movements which were characterized by their anti-bourgeois stance.[1] We do not need to examine the extensive history of these movements in order to identify the principal conceptual feature of Lukács's analysis, namely the opposition between the isolated particular and the all-encompassing totality, and – in Lukács's account – the aim of creating an art which can depict the totality.

Lukács takes as the basis of his analysis the opposition in literature between the avant-garde and realism:

> So-called avant-garde literature [. . .] from Naturalism to Surrealism. What is its general thrust? We may briefly anticipate our findings here by saying that its main trend is its growing distance from, and progressive dissolution of, realism.[2]

Lukács disputes the claim of the avant-garde to be progressive and anti-bourgeois. He does so by asserting the importance of the notion of totality, quoting Marx's claim that capitalism has organized the world as a single, total market:

> Marx says: 'The relations of production of every society form a whole.' [. . .] According to Marx, the decisive progressive role of the bourgeoisie in history is to develop the world market, thanks to which the economy of the whole world becomes an objectively unified totality. (p. 31)

However, because of the continuing crises of capitalism, which is held to be fraught with contradiction, people do not experience capitalism as a unity in consciousness, but are conscious of an appearance of disintegration. Lukács is utilizing Hegelian vocabulary to analyse the discrepancy between the totality and the particular, which he here calls the *essence* and the *appearance*. Capitalism is in *essence* a totality, but may *appear* to the individual consciousness as fragmentary and incoherent. Now, in order to oppose capitalism, it is necessary to be conscious of it, and literature has a role in revealing the nature of reality. Lukács claims that Expressionist and Surrealist literature, which prioritizes dreams, games, the irrational and the purely subjective, is not able to present the reality of capitalism as totality. Only realism can do this. Again it is the vocabulary, of essence (objective totality) and appearance (subjective fragment), which stands out here:

> If literature is a particular form by means of which objective reality is reflected, then it becomes of crucial importance for it to grasp that reality as it truly is, and not to confine itself to reproducing whatever manifests itself immediately and on the surface. If a writer strives to represent reality as it truly is, i.e. if he is an authentic realist, then the question of totality plays a decisive role, no matter how the writer actually conceives the problem intellectually. (p. 33)

Again, we notice that Lukács phrases the matter of understanding capitalism in terms of an opposition between surface particular and global totality. What we should also notice is that last qualification: that the intellectual position of the writer is immaterial. What matters for the purpose of the political assessment of the role and nature of art is the *form* of the art-work and not the *ideological position* of the writer. Of course, it could be argued that Lukács has to downplay the importance of the ideological position of the author because the authors he seeks to defend are, in the vocabulary of that time, 'bourgeois' authors – authors who in no way share the Marxist or communist agenda. This would be to misunderstand Lukács's analysis. Much as Marx had shifted his emphasis from ideology (held to influence people with false ideas) to the commodity (held to confront people with a misleading appearance), so too does Lukács attempt to shift the emphasis from the ideas expressed in literature to its form.

This shift to an emphasis on the formal properties of literature of course assumes that formal and ideological properties can be clearly distinguished, an issue that is politely elided in the work of many more recent commentators who have preferred a type of mixed formal/ideological commentary usually designed to show that the author is either a blessed being or a cursed one, depending ultimately on ideological alignment. The relevance of Lukács's comments on modernism – which are of course negative – emerge very clearly once we turn to the work of Adorno and Benjamin, who, after the example of Lukács, see a challenge for the theorization of art (and of political consciousness in general) in Marx's theory of the commodity, and not in his earlier theory of ideology.

This introduction via the work of Marx and Lukács gives us the necessary context to read the work of Benjamin and Adorno in terms of its implicit framework. It also shows why so many readers of modernism have looked across to the work of these German-language authors to supply a theory of modernity and an accompanying aesthetic theory which English-language writers and theoreticians of the period were simply unable to attain. This in turn reminds us that Anglo-American modernism as a whole (if not in all of its parts) seemed to have a different centre of gravity to its continental equivalents. Yet what Adorno and Benjamin found to praise in modernism certainly finds its equivalent moments in that segment of modernist history which concerns us here.

In the 1920s, Walter Benjamin found much to endorse in the project of literary Surrealism, a movement with no parallel in Britain or the US, though with imitators in Britain in the 1930s, particularly David Gascoyne. It is a strand in literary history that has been somewhat eclipsed by the casting of the 1930s as the age of W. H. Auden and his circle. If we compare Gascoyne's *A Short Survey of Surrealism* (1935) to Benjamin's 'Surrealism: The Last Snapshot of the European Intelligentsia' (1929),[3] we immediately note the contrast between Gascoyne, who attempts a plain summary of the general tenets of Surrealism following manifestos by the Surrealist leader André Breton and others, and Benjamin, who claims at the opening of his essay that Surrealism can be more meaningfully grasped by a German critic than in its original French context. By this he means that the context of German-language philosophy and intellectual history can place Surrealism more accurately in the context of revolution than it itself managed to do. In Benjamin's own words: 'Intellectual currents can generate a sufficient head of water for the critic to install his power station on them. The necessary gradient, in the case of Surrealism, is produced by the difference in intellectual level between France and Germany' (p. 205).

Benjamin's approach is always to attempt to identify the situation of the art-work *within* the network of social relations that constitute capitalism, rather than asking what the art-work has to say *about* capitalism. This is better expressed in his own words in his 1934 address to the Institute for the Study of Fascism in Paris, called 'The Author as Producer':

> Rather than asking, 'What is the attitude of a work *to* the relations of production of its time?' I would like to ask, 'What is its position *in* them?' This question directly concerns the function the work has within the literary relations of production of its time. It is concerned, in other words, directly with the literary *technique* of works.[4]

This emphasis on technique does not imply that Benjamin wishes for a rigorous formal appraisal of works. Rather, he is emphasizing this notion of the form and social situation of a literary or other aesthetic artefact in order to get away from the demand – which grew as Fascism itself grew – that authors and other artists should be judged by their social commitment, and should use their art to serve up pro-communist positions or be judged as 'ideological', that is, on the side of capitalism due to their mystification of reality.

Benjamin, like Lukács, resists the claim of politically urgent times that a work must be judged by the author's known or stated political position, in favour of an assessment of the structure of a work in terms of its mode of insertion into reality and its effects on the reality around it; not least, its effect on consciousness. This assessment in turn leads to reflection on the tendency of a literary or artistic form towards either enhancing or inhibiting the revolutionary conscious-ness of the working class. This approach enables Benjamin to go beyond the classical forms of art and writing and propose an analysis of the newspaper as a form of writing in which the reader 'is at all times ready to become a writer [. . .] he gains access to authorship'.[5] It also enables Benjamin to produce an analysis of the social function of photography and film, two clearly non-classical art forms, in his famous essay 'The Work of Art in the Age of its Technological Repro-ducibility' (1936).[6] Moreover, it means that in the context of the avant-garde, notably Surrealism, Benjamin has an approach which can analyse the literary artefacts Surrealism produced not merely as different variants of a fixed entity known as literature, but as a new type of literature with a new social function:

> At the outset [. . .] Breton declared his intention of breaking with a praxis that presents the public with the literary precipitate of a certain form of existence while withholding that existence itself. [. . .] The writings of this circle are not literature but something else – demonstra-tions, watchwords, documents, bluffs, forgeries if you will, but at any rate not literature.[7]

As theorized by Breton, this is an anti-literature concerned with inserting texts in to social reality in such a way as to alter the nature of life. This emphasis on the locatedness of the text corresponds to Marx's emphasis on the nature of the commodity – and a complicat-ing feature in the analysis of any art will be that the products of art tend to become commodities and must in part be analysed as such. What Benjamin finds in the Surrealist text is an anti-capitalist art which does not defeat capitalism by *explaining* it, but by *interrupting* it.

The emphasis on the fragmentary interruption is the exact contrary of Lukács's insistence on a literature which provides a total vision. Benjamin uses the phrase 'profane illumination' to characterize the visionary, but not religious, moment of realization which Surrealist experience can grant. According to his account, the materiality of the image and of the word are restored in Surrealist practice, and it is mean-ing itself – normally the *deferral* of materiality – which is held at bay:

Life seemed worth living only where the threshold between waking and sleeping was worn away in everyone as by the steps of multitudinous images flooding back and forth; language seemed itself only where sound and image, image and sound, interpenetrated with automatic precision and such felicity that no chink was left for the penny-in-the-slot called 'meaning'. Image and language take precedence. (p. 208)

Benjamin wishes to link this restoration of immediacy to revolutionary practice:

To win the energies of intoxication for the revolution – this is the project on which Surrealism focuses in all its books and enterprises.

In the joke too, in invective, in misunderstanding, in all cases where an action puts forth its own image and exists, absorbing and consuming it, where nearness looks with its own eyes, the long-sought image space is opened, the world of universal and integral actualities, where the 'best room' is missing – the space, in a word, in which political materialism and physical creatureliness share the inner man, the psyche, the individual, or whatever else we wish to throw to them, with dialectical justice, so that no limb remains untorn. Nevertheless – indeed, precisely after such a dialectical annihilation – this will still be an image space and, more concretely, a body space. [. . .] The collective is a body, too. And the physis [nature] that is being organized for it in technology can, through all its political and factual reality, be produced only in that image space to which profane illumination initiates us. (pp. 215, 217)

This quotation – which has more ramifications than can be thoroughly explored here – has a plain connection to the concerns of Romanticism, via Marx. This 'image space', where 'nearness looks with its own eyes', is a world of 'actualities': the actual, the real, material nature which capitalism and its commodity culture have deferred. The gap with nature can be closed by revolutionary practice.

In the specific notion he develops of the restoration of nature, Benjamin creates an interesting extension of the Romantic idea that society has lost nature (which he confirms as a lost immediacy of language and of image). Moreover, he finds a way to talk about technology, in its role as the social mediator of nature, and about consciousness or experience – or something that neither of those terms covers, the opening of what he calls a 'body space' of newly authentic, post-revolutionary existence.

All of this is at stake in Benjamin's justly celebrated (though perhaps occasionally underinterpreted) essay on photography and film, 'The Work of Art in the Age of its Technological Reproducibility'.[8] Marx had argued that the projected future state of communism depended for its possibility on the productive technologies created and fostered by capitalism, technologies that enabled an unprecedented degree of human freedom through their domination of nature. In this respect, Marx argued, capitalism was its own grave-digger; that is, capitalism was a transitory stage on the way to an inevitable communist future. In his essay, Benjamin claims that the technology of capitalism has implications not only for the level of human wealth, but also for the structure of human consciousness and experience. Marx had not attempted to produce a theory of culture and consciousness: that is what Benjamin attempts.

Throughout the essay, Benjamin's underlying model depends in one way or another on the Hegelian opposition between totality and particularity. While Lukács, in his account of the modern novel, stressed the importance of a total perspective which the novel could bring in its portrayal of the social whole, Benjamin does not even remotely address the question of the ideological content of films – a major issue, as the Nazis came to use cinema as part of their propaganda machine. Rather, he concentrates on the technology of cinema and the effects of film's way of showing on the structure of consciousness. He argues that film is akin to avant-garde art, in terms of its power to shock consciousness and thereby disrupt the influence of ideology and the prison of everyday life.

Reflecting communist ideas of the day, ideas which had grown up in response to the urgency of opposing Nazism, Benjamin claims that photography and film will challenge the remote elitism of traditional art by putting things into the hands of the masses, by bringing them closer. He famously discusses this in terms of the loss of 'aura':

> What, then, is the aura? A strange tissue of space and time: the unique apparition of a distance, however near it may be. To follow with the eye – while resting on a summer afternoon – a mountain range on the horizon or a branch that casts its shadow on the beholder is to breathe the aura of those mountains, of that branch. In the light of this description, we can readily grasp the social basis of the aura's present decay.

It rests on two circumstances, both linked to the increasing emergence of the masses and the growing intensity of their movements. Namely: *the desire of the present day masses to 'get closer' to things, and their equally passionate desire for overcoming each thing's uniqueness by assimilating it as a reproduction.* Every day the urge grows stronger to get hold of an object at close range in an image, or, better, in a facsimile, a reproduction.[9]

On the one hand, this passage suggests that power is being put into the hands of the masses, and adopts a vocabulary that would have found resonance at the time, suggesting that the new technology responds to a demand of the 'masses'. Yet just as Benjamin makes an argument *for* the technology of photography and film as bringing reality closer and demystifying it, we note that the terms of his argument quietly suggest the opposite – that the notion of bringing things (the particular, nature) closer is as illogical as the notion that one should demystify a charming landscape by removing its aura and mystery and 'bringing it closer'. What does it mean for humanity to conquer nature by bringing 'each thing's uniqueness' closer, submitting it to human thought by making everything into a reproduction, not a unique original at all?

Benjamin only implies this question, in an ambivalent moment in a text which seems otherwise intended to celebrate the tendency of the technology of representation to liberate the masses from bourgeois ideology and prepare for a communist future – an optimistic argument in 1936, as the Nazis moved to destroy communism in Germany. Alongside one question, about whether the consciousness of the masses can be liberated by the very structure of the technology which capitalism has developed, Benjamin hints at another question, one already familiar to his contemporaries: will human reason and technology come to dominate nature so far that nothing of 'nature' is left? Will reason come to dominate life so far that everything is turned into knowledge and instrumentalized for human ends?

Of course, the possibility that reason and human ends could destroy contact with nature is one of the central themes of Romanticism, in one form or other. William Wordsworth wrote:

> The world is too much with us; late and soon,
> Getting and spending, we lay waste our powers:
> Little we see in nature that is ours;
> We have given our hearts away, a sordid boon![10]

We can find a similar sentiment in many tracts of the work of Lawrence. However, Romantics and modernists in England were never in a position to give this node of thought the highly elaborated treatment which it was given in the German tradition, and for this reason students of modernism will frequently turn to the work of Adorno, and to his collaboration with Max Horkheimer on *Dialectic of Enlightenment* (1944).

Dialectic of Enlightenment gives a speculative account of modernity as a terrifying realization of the process of European Enlightenment – a process given its name in the eighteenth century, although arguably begun earlier:

> In the most general sense of progressive thought, the Enlightenment has always aimed at liberating men from fear and establishing their sovereignty. Yet the fully enlightened earth radiates disaster triumphant. The program of the Enlightenment was the disenchantment of the world: the dissolution of myths and the substitution of knowledge for fancy. [...] Knowledge, which is power, knows no obstacles: neither in the enslavement of men nor in compliance with the world's rulers. [...] Technology is the essence of this knowledge. It does not work by concepts and images, by the fortunate insight, but refers to method, the exploitation of others' work, and capital. [...] What men want to learn from nature is how to use it in order wholly to dominate it and other men.[11]

On the one hand, people have to work to dominate nature because otherwise it will dominate them – they will be dependent on it, unable to resist famine and flood, and unable therefore to assert human freedom. In the process of becoming independent of nature, people learn not to fear its forces but to harness them towards human ends. However, the technology which enables this domination of nature also brings about a domination of people, and the emphasis on knowledge as an instrument of domination increasingly makes human life instrumental, rather than an end in itself. A process of domination extends throughout human society, both in the inner life of the individual and in every aspect of collective and interpersonal life.

This starting point allows for a powerful analysis of culture, and contrasts with the more common varieties of cultural pessimism found at this time, which highlighted the decline of religion, the end of traditional rural society, and the increasing fragmentation of society into specialized subclasses – a pessimism which Adorno and Horkheimer could note in Germany, and which also characterizes various forms of cultural pessimism in England, such as that of Eliot and F. R. Leavis. Even Lewis, who commented frequently on the standardization process of cultural technology, did not achieve the sweeping oversight which Adorno's commentary on the culture industry was able to bring:

> The sociological theory that the loss of the support of objectively established religion, the dissolution of the last remnants of precapitalism, together with technological and social differentiation or specialization, have led to cultural chaos is disproved every day: for culture now impresses the same stamp upon everything. Films, radio, and magazines make up a system which is uniform as a whole and in every part. Even the aesthetic activities of political opposites are one in their enthusiastic obedience to the rhythm of the iron system.[12]

This excerpt comes from a fascinating chapter called 'The Culture Industry: Enlightenment as Mass Deception', containing a wonderful speculative foray into all aspects of the culture industry, including the changes to the nature of high art which, along with the mass-produced item, is prevented from realizing the human potential for freedom and individuality to which it alludes. The force of Adorno's approach, in this chapter and throughout his work, is that it is no longer relevant to comment on the ideology of an art-work, as if the art-work contained ideas that influenced society, somehow, from the outside. Rather, it is shown to be essential to analyse the overall process of art-works – and not merely of the classical but of new literary and artistic forms and other forms of organized leisure such as sport.

Adorno's writing is full of acidic, aphoristic comments intended to provoke analysis and to challenge the reality which is ranged against them. 'Amusement under late capitalism is the prolongation of work' (p. 137), he writes, bringing to a pithy head his onslaught on the conventional notion that after work finishes one is a 'free' operative in one's 'own' time, an 'individual' liberated from the factory and the machine. Instead the same forms of organization which control labour time are set to work in leisure time as well, as the individual passes leisure time in the darkened cinema, barking with sadistic laughter at comic violence. This sadistic laughter is actually masochistic, since the cinema-goer in effect laughs by proxy at the violence which is inflicted on himself. Think of how concealed TV cameras in our own time are used to riotous effect to humiliate others – who are then asked to join in with the laughter at their own humiliation, as if to suggest that subservience is ultimately OK. As Adorno writes: 'What all these things have in common is the self-derision of man' (p. 47).

In stressing the psychological mechanisms exploited by the culture industry, Adorno attempts to harness Sigmund Freud to Marx and force insights into the psychic changes – not merely the changes in people's 'ideas' – which are brought about under late capitalism. Throughout, the governing model is that of the general and particular, which we have already noted to be so important for Marx and for Benjamin. In Adorno's account, the dialectic of general and particular has been suspended – this is the tragedy of Enlightenment. Rather than the individual finding a freedom within the totality of society, the society of the Enlightenment has arrived at a totalizing unity on which the individual cannot act: now, the individual must merely submit to the society which is too massive and well organized to be challenged, and must learn to take masochistic pleasure in his own submission.

Is such pessimism warranted? Should we prefer the optimistic strand of Benjamin's essay on technology (ignoring his quietly signalled reservations)? The point of those who bring Hegel, Marx, Lukács, Benjamin and Adorno to the table around which the readers of Anglo-American modernism are seated is that the (undeniably questionable) model of totality and particular has yielded a way of thinking about the human and nature which is an essential intellectual complement to the reading of that literature. These writers are available to us in a full context and meaning as they were not to most of the Anglophone modernists who attempted to think and work through the mechanisms of late capitalism.

CHAPTER 10

The Poststructuralist Inflection

In the previous chapter I explained how certain aspects of the study of modernism and modernity have been made available to us not directly from the texts which constitute English-language modernism, but from parallel developments in the tradition of German thought, which have only more recently become known in the English-speaking world. As well as these thinkers in the German tradition, the reading of modernism in our own time has been greatly advanced, greatly enhanced, by the radical developments in French thinking which took place during and after the 1960s. At this time there was an intense growth in France of attention to the nature of textuality itself, which began with a focus on the structural analysis of texts – structuralism – and migrated into something which American commentators named poststructuralism, a term not adopted in France but one which is useful to designate the manner in which structuralist thought became transmuted into something else. The notable thing about poststructuralist thought was its intense focus on the nature of text, a focus which was developed in part in response to certain texts of French literary modernism. It is not enough to say that our reading of literary modernism was simply 'enhanced' by this intellectual current, more accurate to say that it was revolutionized. More even than this; the poststructuralist account of textuality seemed to make visible for the first time features of radical modernist texts which, once we had identified them, *seemed to have been present all along*, even if the proponents of literary modernism had never discussed their work in these terms. It seems undeniable that what is revealed by poststructuralist reading is not simply an artful speculation imposed belatedly, but something fundamental yet previously invisible that has now been uncovered as if for the first time.

A key figure in this movement has been Jacques Derrida, whose work provides part of the explicit or implicit background of a great deal of recent comment on literary modernism. Derrida's work is of a notable complexity, but the most influential strand in his thinking can be readily summarized. In a number of his early works – *Speech and Phenomena* (1967), *Of Grammatology* (1967), *Writing and Difference* (1967), *Margins of Philosophy* (1972) and *Dissemination* (1972) – Derrida gives an account of theories of language which demonstrates how often language is supposed, by its analysts, to be secondary to the 'real' world. Theories of language, of whatever period and whatever level of sophistication, tend to presuppose that language is secondary to reality, as if the world could appear without it, and as if textuality of any kind could be referred back to an origin in the intention of a speaker (or author), or referred back mechanically to the reality to which it refers. Derrida argues that this presents a problem which philosophy and literature do not properly acknowledge. All thought appears in language, and has an irreducible difficulty in reflecting on that which is not itself, that which is not language. In general, Derrida invites us, though a series of arguments and also a series of literary manoeuvres in his own texts, to embrace the reality that textuality – language in all of its forms – can never fully and properly be referred back to an originating reality, but exists in a constant and elusive state of migration from any origin. Words can never be matched back to things or to any authorial intention, but instead exist in a state of permanent displacement which we must acknowledge even though it cannot be simply grasped conceptually, because, as Derrida argues, this displacement – he calls it *différance* – is not really a concept at all: it is a founding feature of language which can only be hinted at by words but which cannot appear in language since it is prior to any possible linguistic utterance.

Derrida did not invent this notion of the (partial) autonomy of textuality, but inherited it from structuralism. The key tenet of structuralism was that literary texts (a main but not exclusive focus of structuralist thought) should not be analysed in terms of the author's intentions, but in terms of the form of the work itself. More than this, structuralism shifted the focus from the individual work to the way in which language itself produced meaning, both in the context of a work and in the context of the production of social meaning in general – hence the emphasis on textuality rather than on the work. The actuality of language is not bound by the limits of the form of the work in which it appears; rather, language always exceeds the work because it belongs to a network of textuality which extends socially and historically beyond the work and into the society.

If Derrida did not invent this notion, he did give it amazing force in his elaboration of the possible implications that flow from it. The attraction of thinking of language in terms of textuality, rather than in terms of authorial intention or the form of the literary work, seemed extremely obvious to readers of modernism in particular. It is worth pausing to inquire why this might have been so.

The notion of the author as a kind of genius became firmly established in the nineteenth century. The fundamentally Romantic notion of the author, as Poet or genius, was what the Russian formalists and after them the French structuralists reacted against. So strong is the reaction against this notion that it is worth reminding ourselves why it was ever needed. In earlier chapters we have mentioned that many modernist writers were still indebted to the Romantic notion of the Poet or genius, a notion already problematic in that the literary author was increasingly refused reverential treatment.

Why did the Romantics need the notion of genius (archetypally applied to Shakespeare) or of the Poet (William Wordsworth's favoured term)? These cognate ideas were a response to the increasing scientism of the eighteenth century. In fact it was the philosopher René Descartes (1596–1650) who had directed modern thinking towards a vision of mind as fundamentally separate from matter. In doing so, he was instrumental in the creation of modern thought itself, in a break from pre-modern philosophy's Aristotelian and scholastic basis. In his *Meditations on First Philosophy* (1641), Descartes described a dualism between *res cogitans* (thinking substance, or *mind*) and *res extensa* (extended substance, or *matter*). The dualism of mind and matter left the world a profoundly disenchanted place, in that human continuity with nature appears to be lost. The relationship between mind and matter has many cognates, equivalent or parallel dualisms, including that of society and nature and that of language and reality. These dualisms only present a problem to anyone who wants to find a unifying principle in reality. Immanuel Kant (1724–1804) appeared to compound these difficulties in the very attempt to resolve them, by producing an account in his *Critique of Pure Reason* (1781) and *Critique of Practical Reason* (1788) in which he scrupulously separated the domain of human moral choice from that of the mechanical world of nature.

How was the breach between society and nature, or between mind and matter, to be closed? In the German tradition, responses to the dilemma brought to a fine realization by Kant are to be found in the work of Johann Gottlieb Fichte (1762–1814) and Friedrich von Schelling (1775–1854), and following them in the work of G. W. F. Hegel, whose *Phenomenology of Spirit* (1807) is an astounding and profoundly influential attempt to show that mind and matter, society and nature, humankind and world, tend towards a unity in a final moment of what he termed 'absolute knowledge', despite their original separation.

In the English-language tradition, the most prominent attempt to demonstrate a possible unity of man and nature is to be found in the *Prelude* of Wordsworth, completed in 1805 and revised up until 1850, but not published until after his death. In the *Prelude*, Wordsworth attempts to establish himself as the Poet, a man whose moral education has come principally from nature rather than society:

> Wisdom and Spirit of the universe!
> Thou Soul that art the Eternity of Thought!
> That giv'st to forms and images a breath
> And everlasting motion! not in vain,
> By day or star-light thus from my first dawn
> Of Childhood didst Thou intertwine for me
> The passions that build up our human Soul
> Not with the mean and vulgar works of Man,
> But with high objects, with enduring things,
> With life and nature, purifying thus
> The elements of feeling and of thought,
> And sanctifying by such discipline
> Both pain and fear, until we recognize
> A grandeur in the beatings of the heart.[1]

The figure of the Poet is an example of the author as a kind of genius. In fact in Wordsworth's case the emphasis is much more on the Poet than on poetry, which is merely the product of the privileged being who is the Poet. Notice how Wordsworth emphasizes that his being as a youth was formed by nature and not by the 'mean and vulgar works of man'. This assertion – one that cannot really be proved – is made to overcome the possibility of being formed merely by society, independently of nature. Loosely, Wordsworth claims that God is the creator of this nature, in an attempt to ground his theological or ontological claim.

Wordsworth goes on to assert the primacy of imagination as the place where nature and mind meet in freedom. His account of this is not as philosophically elaborated as that of his friend and mentor Samuel Taylor Coleridge, who was immersed in the works of the German Romantics, and who formulated a famous account of imagination in his *Biographia Literaria* (1817):

> The IMAGINATION then, I consider either as primary, or secondary. The primary IMAGINATION I hold to be the living Power and prime Agent of all human Perception, and as the repetition in the finite mind of the eternal act of creation in the infinite I AM. The secondary Imagination I consider as the echo of the former, co-existing with the conscious will, yet still as identical with the primary in the *kind* of its agency, differing only in *degree*, and in the *mode* of its operation. It dissolves, diffuses, dissipates, in order to re-create; or where this process is rendered impossible, yet still at all events it struggles to idealize and to unify. It is essentially *vital*, even as all objects (*as* objects) are essentially fixed and dead.[2]

The first kind of imagination is the power of synthesizing one's impressions of the world. The importance of this claim is that perceptions do not consist of merely mechanical impressions on the various senses. The human mind is not a merely mechanical receptor, but an active and synthesizing one. The possession of the imagination is held to be a god-like quality. The secondary imagination is the creative or productive power: a power of synthesis and creation which, again, transcends the merely mechanical world, and enables the production of an art which is not merely beautiful according to prescribed rules of beauty (themselves arithmetic and mechanical) but which is sublime – the art of genius.

The purpose of this inevitably compressed account of Romantic notions of imagination and poetry is to show how the discrepancy between, or what I prefer to call the non-identity of, mind and matter (and its various cognates) had come to be regarded as a problem, and how thinkers in literature as well as philosophy produced responses to this problem which culminated, among other things, in the assertion of the role of imagination. This assertion turned into an emphasis on the importance of the author as the source and origin of the literary text, and it is this emphasis which structuralism, influenced by a new focus on language itself, sought to correct.

Easily the most famous text in the structuralist venture, and in the modification of structuralism into what we have called poststructuralism, is Roland Barthes's frequently anthologized essay 'The Death of the Author'. Barthes argues that writing must be treated not as the point at which the intention of the author is made manifest, but as the point where the author disappears:

> Writing is the destruction of every voice, of every point of origin. Writing is that neutral, composite, oblique space where our subject slips away, the negative where all identity is lost, starting with the very identity of the body writing.[3]

He vociferously rejects the commonplace focus on the author as origin of the text:

> The image of literature to be found in ordinary culture is tyrannically centred on the author, his person, his life, his tastes, his passions, while criticism still consists for the most part in saying that Baudelaire's work is the failure of Baudelaire the man, Van Gogh's his madness, Tchaikovsky's his vice. The *explanation* of a work is always sought in the man or woman who produced it. (p. 143)

Barthes's example of a writer who attempted to break away from authorship into writing is Stéphane Mallarmé.

> In France, Mallarmé was doubtless the first to see and foresee in its full extent the necessity to substitute language itself for the person who until then had been supposed to be its owner. For him, for us too, it is language which speaks, not the author; to write is, through a prerequisite impersonality, to reach that point where language only acts, 'performs', and not 'me'. Mallarmé's entire poetics consists in suppressing the author in the interests of writing (which is [. . .] to restore the place of the reader). (p. 143)

T. S. Eliot, Ezra Pound and James Joyce were among the first to bring the doctrine of impersonality, and the concept of language as 'performance' or 'enunciation', into literature in English. Compare the opening of 'The Love Song of J. Alfred Prufrock', with its elusive shifting of pronominal responsibilities: 'Let us go then, you and I'.

This dislocation of the word from any imagined voice which gives it articulation is characteristic of modernism. As Barthes points out, once we no longer conceive of writing as being the transcribed utterance of the author, once we no longer imagine that authorial intention holds together everything we read, much as the will of God is held to determine every word in the Bible, the nature of the modern text is entirely transformed:

> Linguistics has recently provided the destruction of the Author with a valuable analytical tool by showing that the whole of the enunciation is an empty process, functioning perfectly without there being any need for it to be filled with the person of the interlocutors. Linguistically, the author is never more than the instance writing, just as *I* is nothing other than the instance saying *I* [. . .].
>
> The removal of the Author [. . .] is not merely an historical fact or an act of writing; it utterly transforms the modern text (or – which is the same thing – the text is henceforth made and read in such a way that at all levels its author is absent). [. . .] The Author, when believed in, is always conceived of as the past of his own book: book and author stand automatically on a single line divided into a *before* and an *after*. The Author is thought to *nourish* the book, which is to say that he exists before it, thinks, suffers, lives for it, is in the same relation of antecedence to his work as a father to his child. In complete contrast, the modern scriptor is born simultaneously with the text, is in no way equipped with a being preceding or exceeding the writing, is not the subject with the book as predicate; there is no other time than that of the enunciation and every text is written *here and now*. (p. 145)

Barthes now speaks not of the author but of the scriptor: the author is held to be a source and origin of meaning; the scriptor is merely someone who writes:

> We know that a text is not a line of words releasing a single 'theological' meaning (the 'message' of the Author-God) but a multi-dimensional

space in which a variety of writings, none of them original, blend and clash. The text is a tissue of quotations drawn from the innumerable centres of culture. [. . .] Succeeding the Author, the scriptor no longer bears within him passions, humours, feelings, impressions, but rather this immense dictionary from which he draws a writing that can know no halt: life never does more than imitate the book, and the book itself is only a tissue of signs, an imitation that is lost, infinitely deferred.

Once the Author is removed, the claim to decipher a text becomes quite futile. To give a text an Author is to impose a limit on that text, to furnish it with a final signified, to close the writing. [. . .] In the multiplicity of writing, everything is to be *disentangled*, nothing *deciphered*; the structure can be followed, 'run' (like the thread of a stocking) at every point and at every level, but there is nothing beneath: the space of writing is to be ranged over, not pierced; writing ceaselessly posits meaning ceaselessly to evaporate it, carrying out a systematic exemption of meaning. (p. 146)

This notion of writing as text carried with it a wholly new approach to reading, one which has proved very stimulating in the context of literary studies in general, and has particular appeal in the context of those modernist works where the complexity of the textual artefact requires a participation which goes beyond the decipherment of authorial intention.

It has been the work of Jacques Derrida which has most notably opened up the possibilities of a productive readerliness, especially in relation to his emphasis – related closely to Barthes's discussion – on the text as a force of permanent dissemination, one which can never be fully or finally recuperated to any originary meaning. The following passage from his essay 'Différance' is particularly influential. *Différance* is a coinage in French which cannot be translated, it is a portmanteau word which combines the notions of spatial differentiation and temporal differentiation. Derrida gives us a graceful and provocative way of thinking about language, not as something which exists in a particular point of time and space, but as something which is deployed through time (as speech) and through space (as writing). For a classical notion of language and the sign, one which claims that meaning is recuperable by reference to the mind of the speaker or to the world which language names, he wishes to substitute the term *différance*, to suggest a way in which we can acknowledge the permanent discrepancy of language and world. In what went before, we have seen that a variety of binary oppositions has been produced in intellectual history which can be regarded as cognates of the opposition between mind and matter insisted on by Descartes. The novelty here, following the modern emphasis on language, is that it is now the sign (language) which makes an appearance in opposition to the world, reality or matter. Grasping his work in this way, we can see that Derrida is very much set to embrace the discrepancy of these dualities not by accepting duality, but by making it appear no longer as a problem but as a peculiar condition in which we ourselves are inscribed, a condition of possibility. Throughout most of this passage from 'Différance', Derrida is characterizing the classical position on language which he rejects:

> *Différance* as temporisation, *différance* as spacing. How are they to be joined?
>
> Let us start, since we are already there, from the problematic of the sign and of writing. The sign is usually said to be put in the place of the thing itself, the present thing, 'thing' here standing equally for meaning or referent. The sign represents the present in its absence. It takes the place of the present. When we cannot grasp or show the thing, state the present, the being-present, when the present cannot be presented, we signify, we go through the detour of the sign. We take or give signs. We signal. The sign, in this sense, is deferred presence. Whether we are concerned with the verbal or the written sign, with the monetary sign, or with electoral delegation and political representation, the circulation of the sign defers the moment in which we can encounter the thing itself, make it ours, consume or expend it, touch it, see it, intuit its presence. What I am describing here in order to define it is the classically determined structure of the sign in all the banality of its characteristics – signification as the *différance* of temporisation. And this structure presupposes that the sign, which defers presence, is conceivable only on the *basis* of the presence that it defers and *moving toward* the deferred presence that it aims to reappropriate. According to this classical semiology, the substitution of the sign for the thing itself is both *secondary* and *provisional*: secondary due to an original and lost presence from which the sign thus derives; provisional as concerns this final and missing presence toward which the sign in this sense is a movement of mediation.

> In attempting to put into question these traits of the provisional secondariness of the substitute, one would come to see something like an originary *différance*; but one could no longer call it originary or final.[4]

Keen readers of Derrida are fond of insisting on the resistance of his work to paraphrase due to its acute rhetorical specificity, but I hope that a tentative gloss will not be too out of order. All I have given here is Derrida's summary account of the classical notion of representation. In it he does not simply summarize those ideas so much as present us with a whole sequence of samples of the rhetoric by which signification is commonly explained. In doing so, he places before us the manner in which these accounts tend to rest on a rhetoric of *presence*, a rhetoric in which it is implicitly or explicitly presumed that the sign is a temporary substitute for the real world which it seems to designate, a reality that could in principle be restored and the sign, as it were, be handed back like an IOU. Against this classical notion, Derrida will go on to develop his own term, *différance*, a term evolved to remind us that signs are not like IOUs which can be handed back in exchange for real things.

Différance has become part of the critical armoury, and has reinforced the art of close textual analysis, not only because it gives a kind of intellectual foundation to the sense of elusiveness which close reading so often produces, but because it maps on to concerns about the nature of voice and language which are inscribed in the atomic structure of the most linguistically self-aware texts. In my discussion of Eliot and modernist reading I have already indicated that a complex groundlessness of reading is a central component of that poet's aesthetic. Conversely, *différance* can lead us to a suspicion of Pound's severely nominalist aesthetics, in which there is a distrust of rhetoric and an attempt to make words more thing-like than their necessarily discursive nature properly allows. I have also outlined how in *Ulysses* love is produced as an elusive ideal of a reconciled totality in a world where mind attempts to grasp body in a chain of desire which I have called, following Sigmund Freud, fetishism – a chain which never leads to complete finality, closure or satisfaction, but in which one must learn to rest where one is. Molly Bloom's final monologue closes with a remarkable and ambiguous celebration of her love for her husband. We conclude from these closing words that Molly is thinking about Bloom as she falls asleep, affirming her love for him despite her day's infidelity. As she falls asleep, passing before her mind the moment in which she decided to accept Bloom, the many instances of her word of acceptance, 'yes', are commented on by a surprising qualification:

> and how he kissed me under the Moorish wall and I thought as well him as another and then I asked him with my eyes to ask again yes and then he asked me would I yes to say yes my mountain flower and first I put my arms around him yes and drew him down to me so he could feel my breasts all perfume yes and his heart was going like mad and yes I said yes I will Yes. (p. 933)

I have commented already in chapter 6 on Joyce's sociological eye for the patterns of courtship. Here Molly, who formally must be asked to marry, in practice elicits the question herself. This is the sociological aspect. Rhetorically, the remarkable detail is the qualification 'as well him as another', suggesting that in the fullness of assent to one particular man, what is really being assented to is assent itself, since the object of love can always in principle be substituted by another. Here the circle is not closed, love does not represent a closure and finality in its consummation, but is a moment in an endless and open process, in which the reciprocal subject and object of love combine not in unity but in endless slippage. Like Derridean *différance*, Joycean love is an acceptance of the dislocatedness of being, in which origins are lost for ever and the purpose of the journey lies in the pleasure of merely circulating.

Notes

CHAPTER 1   H. D., EZRA POUND AND IMAGISM

1 *The Selected Letters of Ezra Pound: 1907–1941*, ed. D. D. Paige (New York: New Directions, 1971), p. 11.

2 T. S. Eliot, *The Sacred Wood: Essays on Poetry and Criticism* (London: Methuen, 1960), pp. 95–103.

3 Peter Jones (ed.), *Imagist Poetry* (Harmondsworth: Penguin, 1972), p. 61.

4 *Select Epigrams from the Greek Anthology*, ed. with a revised text, trans. and notes J. W. Mackail (London: Longmans, Green, 1890), epigram no. XLIII.

5 *Collected Poems: 1912–1944*, ed. Louis L. Martz (New York: New Directions, 1983), p. 309.

6 *Imagist Poetry*, p. 56.

7 Ezra Pound, *Collected Shorter Poems* (London: Faber and Faber, 1968), p. 85.

8 *The Translations of Ezra Pound*, intro. Hugh Kenner (London: Faber and Faber, 1970), pp. 23–4.

9 *Literary Essays of Ezra Pound*, ed. and intro. T. S. Eliot (London: Faber and Faber, 1960), p. 25.

10 *Literary Essays of Ezra Pound*, p. 25.

11 *Collected Shorter Poems*, p. 102.

12 Ezra Pound, *Gaudier-Brzeska: A Memoir* (Hessle: Marvell Press, 1960), p. 89.

13 Ernest Fenollosa, *The Chinese Written Character as a Medium for Poetry*, ed. Ezra Pound (New York: City Lights, 1968), p. 9.

CHAPTER 2   T. S. ELIOT AND MODERNIST READING

1 Martin Heidegger, 'Language', in *Poetry, Language, Thought*, trans. Albert Hofstadter (New York: Harper and Row, 1975), p. 210.
2 Jacques Lacan, *The Four Fundamental Concepts of Psychoanalysis*, ed. Jacques-Alain Miller, trans. Alan Sheridan, intro. David Macey (London: Penguin, 1994), p. 199.
3 In *Collected Poems: 1909–1962* (London: Faber and Faber, 1974), pp. 13–17.
4 Hugh Kenner, *The Invisible Poet: T. S. Eliot* (London: Methuen, 1965), p. 35.
5 *The Sacred Wood: Essays on Poetry and Criticism* (London: Methuen, 1960), p. 53.
6 *The Sacred Wood*, p. 59.

CHAPTER 3   'THE WASTE LAND', NANCY CUNARD AND MINA LOY

1 F. R. Leavis, *New Bearings in English Poetry* (Harmondsworth: Penguin, 1972), p. 71.
2 *The Waste Land: A Facsimile and Transcript of the Original Drafts including the Annotations of Ezra Pound*, ed. Valerie Eliot (London: Faber and Faber, 1971), pp. 4–5. The line is taken from Charles Dickens, *Our Mutual Friend*.
3 See *Ulysses: Annotated Students' Edition*, intro. and notes Declan Kiberd (London: Penguin, 1992), pp. 194 and 212; subsequent references on pp. 542, 610, 629, 819.
4 *Parallax* (Cambridge: Parataxis Editions, 2001), p. 4.
5 Mina Loy, *The Lost Lunar Baedeker* (Manchester: Carcanet, 1997), p. 33.
6 Umbro Apollonio (ed.), *Futurist Manifestos* (London: Thames and Hudson, 1973), pp. 95–106.
7 *Futurist Manifestos*, p. 71.
8 *The Lost Lunar Baedeker*, p. 156.

CHAPTER 4   WALLACE STEVENS AND ROMANTIC LEGACY

1 William Carlos Williams, *Paterson* (New York: New Directions, 1963), p. 6.
2 *Gaudier-Brzeska: A Memoir* (Hessle: Marvell Press, 1960), p. 89.
3 *Collected Poems* (London: Faber and Faber, 1955), p. 127.
4 *William Wordsworth*, ed. Stephen Gill (Oxford and New York: Oxford University Press, 1986), pp. 303–4.
5 *William Wordsworth*, p. 580.
6 *Collected Poems*, p. 92.

7 *Collected Poems*, pp. 128–31.
8 *Moby-Dick*, ed., intro. and commentary Harold Beaver (Harmondsworth: Penguin, 1972), p. 262.

CHAPTER 5   WYNDHAM LEWIS: GENIUS AND ART

1 *The Portable Coleridge*, ed. and intro. I. A. Richards (Harmondsworth: Penguin, 1977), p. 516.
2 *Blast*, 1 (June 1914), 7, 8.
3 *Blast*, 1, 30.
4 *Blast*, 2 (July 1915), 94.
5 *Tarr* (Harmondsworth: Penguin, 1982), p. 45.
6 *Tarr*, p. 314.
7 *Tarr*, p. 78.
8 *Tarr*, pp. 20, 312.

CHAPTER 6   JAMES JOYCE: *ULYSSES* AND LOVE

1 *Selected Prose of T. S. Eliot*, ed. and intro. Frank Kermode (London: Faber and Faber, 1975), p. 178.
2 The former account is enabled by Richard Ellmann, who celebrates Bloom's 'bodiliness' without, however, rejecting spirit, in *Ulysses on the Liffey* (London: Faber and Faber, 1972). The latter is unfolded by Declan Kiberd in his introduction and notes to *Ulysses: Annotated Students' Edition* (London: Penguin, 1992). All references are to this edition.
3 *Dubliners*, intro. and notes Terence Brown (London: Penguin, 1992), p. 211.

CHAPTER 7   D. H. LAWRENCE: JAZZ AND LIFE

1 *The Portable Harlem Renaissance Reader*, ed. and intro. David Levering Lewis (London: Penguin, 1995), p. 260.
2 *Portable Harlem Renaissance Reader*, p. 95.
3 From W. E. B. Du Bois, *Dark Princess: A Romance* (New York: Harcourt Brace, 1928), p. 8; and quoted *Paleface* (London: Chatto and Windus, 1929), p. 30.
4 *Dark Princess*, p. 297.
5 In *Collected Poems: 1909–1962* (London: Faber and Faber, 1974), p. 67.
6 Theodor Adorno, 'Gebrauchsmusik' (1924), in Adorno, *Gesammelte Schriften*, vol. 19, ed. Rolf Tiedemann (Frankfurt: Suhrkamp, 1984), pp. 445–7.

7 'Abschied vom Jazz', in *Gesammelte Schriften*, vol. 18, pp. 795–9.
8 See Adorno, 'On Jazz', tran. Jamie Owen Daniel, in *Discourse: Journal for Theoretical Studies in Media and Culture* 12.1 (Fall–Winter 1989–90), 45–77.
9 *Lady Chatterley's Lover*, ed., intro. and notes Michael Squires (London: Penguin, 1994), p. 300.
10 *Sons and Lovers*, ed., intro. and notes Helen Baron and Carl Baron (London: Penguin, 1994), p. 261.
11 *The Rainbow*, ed. Mark Kinkead-Weekes, intro. and notes Anne Fernihough (London: Penguin, 1995), p. 11.

CHAPTER 8   VIRGINIA WOOLF: ART AND CLASS

1 *A Room of One's Own and Three Guineas*, ed., intro. and notes Michèle Barrett (London: Penguin, 1993), p. 127.
2 Maggie Newbery, *Picking Up Threads: The Complete Reminiscences of a Bradford Mill Girl*, ed. James Ogden (Bradford: Bradford Libraries, 1993). 1st pub. 1980.
3 Barrett in *A Room of One's Own and Three Guineas*, p. x.
4 *To the Lighthouse*, ed. Stella McNichol. intro. and notes Hermione Lee (London: Penguin, 1992), p. 54.
5 Roger Fry, *Vision and Design*, ed. J. B. Bullen (London and New York: Oxford University Press, 1981), pp. 7–8.
6 *Vision and Design*, pp. 23–4, 20.

CHAPTER 9   THE MODERNITY OF ADORNO
AND BENJAMIN

1 This exchange appears in translation in Ernst Bloch et al., *Aesthetics and Politics*, ed. Ronald Taylor, afterword Fredric Jameson (London: New Left Books, 1977), pp. 9–59.
2 *Aesthetics and Politics*, p. 29.
3 Walter Benjamin, *Selected Writings. Vol. 2: 1927–34*, trans. Rodney Livingstone et al., eds Michael W. Jennings, Howard Eiland and Gary Smith (Cambridge, MA, and London: Harvard University Press, 1999), pp. 207–18.
4 *Selected Writings. Vol. 2*, p. 770.
5 'The Newspaper', in *Selected Writings. Vol. 2*, p. 741.
6 This essay has appeared under a misleadingly translated title: 'The Work of Art in the Age of Mechanical Reproduction'.
7 *Selected Writings. Vol. 2*, pp. 207–8.

8 *Selected Writings. Vol. 3: 1935–1938*, trans. Edmund Jephcott, Howard Eiland et al., eds Howard Eiland and Michael W. Jennings (Cambridge, MA, and London: Harvard University Press, 2002), pp. 101–22.
9 *Selected Writings. Vol. 3*, pp. 104–5. Italics in original.
10 Stephen Gill (ed.), *William Wordsworth* (Oxford: Oxford University Press, 1984), p. 270.
11 *Dialectic of Enlightenment*, trans. John Cumming (London: Verso, 1979), pp. 3–4.
12 *Dialectic of Enlightenment*, p. 120.

CHAPTER 10   THE POSTSTRUCTURALIST INFLECTION

1 The *Prelude*, in *William Wordsworth*, ed. Stephen Gill (Oxford: Oxford University Press, 1984), pp. 385–6.
2 *The Portable Coleridge*, ed. and intro. I. A. Richards (Harmondsworth: Penguin, 1977), p. 516.
3 Roland Barthes, *Image, Music, Text*, selected and trans. Stephen Heath (London: Fontana, 1977), p. 142.
4 *Margins of Philosophy*, trans. and additional notes Alan Bass (London: Harvester Press, 1982), p. 9.

Bibliography

GENERAL

Armstrong, Tim, *Modernism, Technology and the Body: A Cultural Study*. Cambridge: Cambridge University Press, 1998.

Ayers, David, *English Literature of the 1920s*. Edinburgh: Edinburgh University Press, 1999.

Benstock, Shari, *Women of the Left Bank: Paris, 1900–1940*. London: Virago, 1987.

Berman, Marshall, *All That is Solid Melts Into Air: The Experience of Modernity*. London: Verso, 1983.

Bradbury, Malcolm and James McFarlane (eds), *Modernism: A Guide to European Literature: 1890–1930*. London: Penguin, 1991.

Butler, Christopher, *Early Modernism: Literature Music and Painting in Europe: 1900–1916*. Oxford: Clarendon Press, 1994.

Carey, John, *The Intellectuals and the Masses*. London: Faber and Faber, 1992.

Dowson, Jane, *Women, Modernism and British Poetry, 1910–1939: Resisting Femininity*. Burlington, VT: Ashgate, 2002.

Goldman, Jane, *Modernism, 1910–1945: Image to Apocalypse*. Houndmills, Basingstoke; New York: Palgrave Macmillan, 2004.

Kenner, Hugh, *The Pound Era: The Age of Ezra Pound, T. S. Eliot, James Joyce and Wyndham Lewis*. London: Faber and Faber, 1972.

Levenson, Michael H., *A Genealogy of Modernism: A Study of English Literary Doctrine 1908–1922*. Cambridge: Cambridge University Press, 1984.

Nicholls, Peter, *Modernisms: A Literary Guide*. London: Macmillan, 1995.

North, Michael, *Reading 1922: A Return to the Scene of the Modern*. New York and Oxford: Oxford University Press, 1999.

Stevenson, Randall, *Modernist Fiction: An Introduction*. New York and London: Harvester Wheatsheaf, 1992.

Tratner, Michael, *Modernism and Mass Politics: Joyce, Woolf, Eliot and Yeats*. Stanford, CA: Stanford University Press, 1995.

Trotter, David, *Paranoid Modernism: Literary Experiment, Psychosis and the Professionalization of English Society*. Oxford: Oxford University Press, 2001.

CHAPTER 1   H. D., EZRA POUND AND IMAGISM

Bell, Ian F. A., *Critic as Scientist: The Modernist Poetics of Ezra Pound*. London: Methuen, 1981.

Brooker, Peter, *A Students' Guide to the Selected Poems of Ezra Pound*. London: Faber and Faber, 1979.

Carpenter, Humphrey, *A Serious Character: The Life of Ezra Pound*. London: Faber and Faber, 1988.

Davie, Donald, *Ezra Pound: Poet as Sculptor*. London: Routledge and Kegan Paul, 1965.

Ellmann, Maud, *The Poetics of Impersonality: T. S. Eliot and Ezra Pound*. Brighton: Harvester Press, 1987.

H. D., *Bid Me to Live*. London: Virago, 1984.

H. D., *Collected Poems: 1912–1944*. Ed. Louis L. Martz. New York: New Directions, 1983.

H. D., *Trilogy*. New York: New Directions, 1973.

Jones, Peter (ed.), *Imagist Poetry*. Harmondsworth: Penguin, 1972.

Kenner, Hugh, *The Pound Era: The Age of Ezra Pound, T. S. Eliot, James Joyce and Wyndham Lewis*. London: Faber and Faber, 1972.

Nicholls, Peter, *Ezra Pound: Politics, Economics and Writing. A Study of the Cantos*. London: Macmillan, 1984.

Pound, Ezra, *The Cantos*. 4th collected edn. London: Faber and Faber, 1987.

Pound, Ezra, *Collected Early Poems of Ezra Pound*. Ed. Michael John King, intro. Louis L. Martz. London: Faber and Faber, 1977.

Pound, Ezra, *Collected Shorter Poems*. London: Faber and Faber, 1968.

Pound, Ezra, *Gaudier-Brzeska: A Memoir*. Hessle: Marvell Press, 1960.

Pound, Ezra, *Guide to Kulchur*. 1938. London: Peter Owen, 1978.

Pound, Ezra, *Literary Essays of Ezra Pound*. Ed. and intro. T. S. Eliot. 1954. London: Faber and Faber, 1960.

Pound, Ezra, *Selected Prose 1909–1965*. Ed. and intro. William Cookson. London: Faber and Faber, 1973.

Pound, Ezra, *The Translations of Ezra Pound*. Intro. Hugh Kenner. Enlarged edn. London: Faber and Faber, 1970.

Terrell, Carroll F., *A Companion to the Cantos of Ezra Pound*. 2 vols. Berkeley: University of California Press, 1980–4.

CHAPTERS 2 AND 3   T. S. ELIOT, NANCY CUNARD AND MINA LOY

Ackroyd, Peter, *T. S. Eliot: A Life*. New York: Simon and Schuster, 1984.

Bergonzi, Bernard, *T. S. Eliot*. London: Macmillan, 1972.

Burke, Carolyn, *Becoming Modern: The Life of Mina Loy*. New York: Farrar, Straus, and Giroux, 1996.

Bush, Ronald, *T. S. Eliot: A Study in Character and Style*. New York: Oxford University Press, 1983.

Chisholm, Anne, *Nancy Cunard*. London: Sidgwick and Jackson, 1979.

Davidson, Harriet, *T. S. Eliot and Hermeneutics: Absence and Interpretation in 'The Waste Land'*. Baton Rouge and London: Louisiana State University Press, 1985.

Eliot, T. S., *Collected Poems 1909–1962*. London: Faber and Faber, 1974.

Eliot, T. S., *The Sacred Wood: Essays on Poetry and Criticism*. London: Methuen, 1960.

Eliot, T. S., *Selected Essays*. Third enlarged edn. London: Faber and Faber, 1951.

Ford, Hugh D., *Nancy Cunard: Brave Poet, Indomitable Rebel. 1896–1965*. Philadelphia and London: Chilton, 1968.

Gordon, Lyndall, *Eliot's Early Years*. New York: Oxford University Press, 1977.

Kenner, Hugh, *The Invisible Poet: T. S. Eliot*. London: Methuen, 1965.

Moody, A. D., *Thomas Stearns Eliot: Poet*. Cambridge: Cambridge University Press, 1979.

Schreiber, Maeera and Keith Tuma, *Mina Loy: Woman and Poet*. Orono, ME: National Poetry Foundation, 1998

Scofield, Martin, *T. S. Eliot: The Poems*. Cambridge: Cambridge University Press, 1988.

Southam, B. C., *A Guide to the Selected Poems of T. S. Eliot*. London: Faber and Faber, 1977.

CHAPTER 4   WALLACE STEVENS

Bloom, Harold, *Wallace Stevens: The Poems of Our Climate*. Ithaca, NY: Cornell University Press, 1977.

Kermode, Frank, *Wallace Stevens*. Edinburgh: Oliver and Boyd, 1960.

Stevens, Wallace, *Collected Poems*. London: Faber and Faber, 1955.

Stevens, Wallace, *The Necessary Angel: Essays on Reality and the Imagination*. London: Faber and Faber, 1960.

Stevens, Wallace, *Opus Posthumus*. Ed. Samuel French Morse. London: Faber and Faber, 1990.

Vendler, Helen, *On Extended Wings: Wallace Stevens' Longer Poems*. Cambridge, MA, and London: Harvard University Press, 1974.

CHAPTER 5   WYNDHAM LEWIS

Ayers, David, *Wyndham Lewis and Western Man*. London: Macmillan, 1992.

Bridson, D. G., *The Filibuster: A Study of the Political Ideas of Wyndham Lewis*. London: Cassell, 1972.

Du Bois, W. E. Burghardt, *Dark Princess: A Romance*. New York: Harcourt Brace, 1928.

Hulme, T. E., *Speculations: Essays on Humanism and the Philosophy of Art*. Ed. Herbert Read, foreword Jacob Epstein. 1924. London, Henley and Boston: Routledge and Kegan Paul, 1977.

Kenner, Hugh, *Wyndham Lewis*. London: Methuen, 1954.

Lewis, Wyndham, *The Apes of God*. Afterword Paul Edwards. Santa Barbara: Black Sparrow Press, 1981.

Lewis, Wyndham, *The Art of Being Ruled*. Ed., afterword and notes Reed Way Dasenbrock. Santa Rosa: Black Sparrow Press, 1989.

Lewis, Wyndham, *The Childermass*. London: Chatto and Windus, 1928.

Lewis, Wyndham, *The Complete Wild Body*. Ed. Bernard Lafourcade. Santa Barbara: Black Sparrow Press, 1982.

Lewis, Wyndham, *Tarr*. 1918. Revised 1928. Harmondsworth: Penguin, 1982.

Lewis, Wyndham, *Time and Western Man*. 1927. Ed., afterword and notes Paul Edwards. Santa Rosa: Black Sparrow Press, 1993.

Jameson, Fredric, *Fables of Aggression: Wyndham Lewis; The Modernist as Fascist*. Berkeley; Los Angeles and London: University of California Press, 1979.

Wagner, Geoffrey, *Wyndham Lewis: A Portrait of the Artist as the Enemy*. London: Routledge and Kegan Paul, 1957.

CHAPTER 6   JAMES JOYCE

Attridge, Derek (ed.), *The Cambridge Companion to Joyce*. Cambridge: Cambridge University Press, 1990.

Attridge, Derek and Daniel Ferrer (eds), *Post-structuralist Joyce: Essays from the French*. Cambridge: Cambridge University Press, 1984.

Ellmann, Richard, *James Joyce*. Revised edn. New York: Oxford University Press, 1982.

Joyce, James, *Dubliners*. Intro. and notes Terence Brown. London: Penguin, 1992.

Joyce, James, *A Portrait of the Artist as a Young Man*. Ed., intro. and notes Seamus Deane. London: Penguin, 1992.

Joyce, James, *Ulysses: Annotated Students' Edition*. Intro. and notes Declan Kiberd. London: Penguin, 1992.

Kenner, Hugh, *Joyce's Voices*. 1955. New York: Columbia University Press, 1987.

Levin, Harry, *James Joyce: A Critical Introduction*. 1941. Revised edn. New York: New Directions Press, 1960.

MacCabe, Colin, *James Joyce: New Perspectives*. Brighton: Harvester Press, 1982.

Norris, Margot, *The Decentered Universe of 'Finnegans Wake'*. Baltimore: Johns Hopkins University Press, 1976.

CHAPTER 7   D. H. LAWRENCE

Adorno, Theodor, *Essays on Music*. Ed. Richard Leppert. Berkeley: University of California Press, 2002.

Arlen, Michael, *The Green Hat*. London: Collins, 1924.

Bell, Michael, *D. H. Lawrence: Language and Being*. Cambridge: Cambridge University Press, 1991.

Bergson, Henri, *L'Evolution créatrice*. Paris: PUF, 1941.

Bergson, Henri, *Matière et mémoire: essai sur la relation du corps à l' ésprit*. Paris: PUF, 1939.

Brown, Keith (ed.), *Rethinking Lawrence*. Milton Keynes and Philadelphia: Open University Press, 1990.

Ellis, David, *D. H. Lawrence: Dying Game. 1922–1930*. Cambridge: Cambridge University Press, 1998.

Fernihough, Anne, *D. H. Lawrence: Aesthetics and Ideology*. Oxford: Clarendon Press, 1993.

Holderness, Graham, *D. H. Lawrence: History, Ideology and Fiction*. Dublin: Gill and Macmillan, 1982.

Kinkead-Weekes, Mark, *D. H. Lawrence: Triumph to Exile. 1912–1922*. Cambridge: Cambridge University Press, 1996.

Lawrence, D. H., *Aaron's Rod*. Ed. Mara Kalnins, intro. and notes Steve Vine. London: Penguin, 1995.

Lawrence, D. H., *England, My England and Other Stories*. Ed. Bruce Steele, intro. and notes Michael Bell. London: Penguin, 1995.

Lawrence, D. H., *The First Lady Chatterley: The First Version of Lady Chatterley's Lover*. Foreword Frieda Lawrence. Harmondsworth: Penguin, 1973.

Lawrence, D. H., *The Fox; The Captain's Doll; The Ladybird*. Ed. Dieter Mehl, intro. and notes David Ellis. London: Penguin, 1994.

Lawrence, D. H., *Lady Chatterley's Lover. A Propos of 'Lady Chatterley's Lover'*. Ed., intro. and notes Michael Squires. London: Penguin, 1994.

Lawrence, D. H., *The Rainbow*. Ed. Mark Kinkead-Weekes, intro. and notes Anne Fernihough. London: Penguin, 1995.

Lawrence, D. H., *Sons and Lovers*. Ed., intro. and notes Helen Baron and Carl Baron. London: Penguin, 1994.

Lawrence, D. H., *Women in Love*. Eds David Farmer, Lindeth Vasey and John Worthen. intro. and notes Mark Kinkead-Weekes. London: Penguin, 1995.

Leavis, F. R., *D. H. Lawrence, Novelist*. London: Chatto and Windus, 1955.

Levering Lewis, David (ed.), *The Portable Harlem Renaissance Reader*. London: Penguin, 1995.

Lewis, Wyndham, *Paleface: The Philosophy of the 'Melting Pot'*. London: Chatto and Windus, 1929.

McLeod, Sheila, *D. H. Lawrence's Men and Women*. London: Heinemann, 1985.

Nietzsche, Friedrich, *Beyond Good and Evil: Prelude to a Philosophy of the Future*. Trans., intro. and commentary R. J. Hollingdale. Harmondsworth: Penguin, 1973.

Nietzsche, Friedrich, *Thus Spake Zarathustra. A Book for Everyone and No One*. Trans. and intro. R. J. Hollingdale. Harmondsworth: Penguin, 1969.

Nixon, Cornelia, *Lawrence's Leadership Politics and the Turn Against Women*. Berkeley: University of California Press, 1986.

Ruderman, Judith, *D. H. Lawrence and the Devouring Mother: The Search for a Patriarchal Ideal of Leadership*. Durham, NC: Duke University Press, 1984.

Simpson, Hilary, *D. H. Lawrence and Feminism*. London: Croom Helm, 1982.

Smith, Anne (ed.), *Lawrence and Women*. London: Vision Press, 1978.

CHAPTER 8   VIRGINIA WOOLF

Abel, Elizabeth, *Virginia Woolf and the Fictions of Psychoanalysis*. Chicago: University of Chicago Press, 1989.

Bazin, Nancy Topping, *Virginia Woolf and the Androgynous Vision*. New Brunswick, NJ: Rutgers University Press, 1973.

Beer, Gillian, *Virginia Woolf: The Common Ground. Essays by Gillian Beer*. Edinburgh: Edinburgh University Press, 1996.

Bowlby, Rachel, *Feminist Destinations and Further Essays on Virginia Woolf*. Edinburgh: Edinburgh University Press, 1997.

Bowlby, Rachel (ed.), *Virginia Woolf*. London and New York: Longman, 1992.

DeSalvo, Louise, *Virginia Woolf: The Impact of Childhood Sexual Abuse on her Life and Work*. London: Women's Press, 1989.

DiBattista, Maria, *Virginia Woolf's Major Novels: The Fables of Anon*. New Haven, CT, and London: Yale University Press, 1980.

Ferrer, Daniel, *Virginia Woolf and the Madness of Language*. London: Routledge, 1990.

Hussey, Mark, *The Singing of the Real World: The Philosophy of Virginia Woolf's Fiction*. Columbus: Ohio State University Press, 1986.

Hussey, Mark (ed.), *Virginia Woolf and War: Fiction, Reality and Myth*. Syracuse, NY: Syracuse University Press, 1992.

Kapp, Yvonne, *Eleanor Marx*. 2 vols. London: Virago, 1972-1-6.

Lee, Hermione, *The Novels of Virginia Woolf*. London: Methuen, 1977.

Lee, Hermione, *Virginia Woolf*. London: Chatto and Windus, 1996.

Marcus, Jane, *Virginia Woolf and the Languages of Patriarchy*. Bloomington: Indiana University Press, 1987.

Marcus, Laura, *Virginia Woolf*. Plymouth: Northcote House and British Council, 1997.

Minow-Pinkney, Makiko, *Virginia Woolf and the Problem of the Subject*. Brighton: Harvester Press, 1987.

Newbery, Maggie, *Picking Up Threads: The Complete Reminiscences of a Bradford Mill Girl*. Ed. James Ogden. Bradford: Bradford Libraries, 1993. 1st pub. 1980.

Phillips, Kathy J., *Virginia Woolf against Empire*. Knoxville: University of Tennessee Press, 1994.

Roe, Sue, *Writing and Gender: Virginia Woolf's Writing Practice*. Hemel Hempstead: Harvester Wheatsheaf, 1990.

Snaith, Anna, *Virginia Woolf: Public and Private Negotiations*. New York: St Martins, 2000.

Spivak, Gayatri C., 'Unmaking and Making in *To The Lighthouse*', in *In Other Worlds: Essays in Cultural Politics*. London: Methuen, 1987.

Woolf, Virginia, *Jacob's Room*. Ed., intro. and notes Sue Roe. London: Penguin, 1992.

Woolf, Virginia, *Mrs Dalloway*. Ed. Stella McNichol, intro.and notes Elaine Showalter. London: Penguin, 1992.

Woolf, Virginia, *Orlando*. Ed. Brenda Lyons, intro. and notes Sandra M. Gilbert. London: Penguin, 1993.

Woolf, Virginia, *A Room of One's Own and Three Guineas*. Ed., intro. and notes Michèle Barrett. London: Penguin, 1993.

Woolf, Virginia, *To the Lighthouse*. Ed. Stella McNichol, intro. and notes Hermione Lee. London: Penguin, 1992.

Woolf, Virginia, *The Waves*. Ed., intro. and notes Kate Flint. London: Penguin, 1992.

Zwerdling, Alex, *Virginia Woolf and the Real World*. Berkeley: University of California Press, 1986.

CHAPTER 9   LUKÁCS, BENJAMIN AND ADORNO

Adorno, Theodor W., *The Culture Industry: Selected Essays on Mass Culture*. London: Routledge, 1991.

Adorno, Theodor W. and Max Horkheimer, *Dialectic of Enlightenment*. Trans. John Cumming. 1972. London: Verso, 1979.

Arato, Andrew and Eike Gebhardt (eds), *The Essential Frankfurt School Reader*. 1978. New York: Continuum, 1993.

Benjamin, Walter, *Charles Baudelaire: A Lyric Poet in the Era of High Capitalism*. Trans. Harry Zohn. London: New Left Books, 1973.

Benjamin, Walter, *Illuminations*. Ed. and intro. Hannah Arendt, trans. Harry Zohn. 1968. London: Fontana, 1973.

Benjamin, Walter, *One-way Street and other Writings*. Intro. Susan Sontag, trans. Edmund Jephcott and Kinglsey Shorter. London: New Left Books, 1979.

Benjamin, Walter, *The Origin of German Tragic Drama*. Intro. George Steiner, trans. John Osborne. London: New Left Books, 1977.

Benjamin, Walter, *Understanding Brecht*. Intro. Stanley Mitchell, trans. Anna Bostock. London: New Left Books, 1973.

Bloch, Ernst, et al., *Aesthetics and Politics*. Ed. Ronald Taylor, afterword Fredric Jameson. London: New Left Books, 1977.

Bottomore, Tom, *The Frankfurt School*. New York: Tavistock Publications, 1984.

Buck-Morss, Susan, *Dialectics of Seeing: Walter Benjamin and the Arcades Project*. Cambridge, MA, and London: MIT Press, 1991.

Buck-Morss, Susan, *The Origin of Negative Dialectics: Theodor W. Adorno, Walter Benjamin and the Frankfurt Institute*. Hassocks: Harvester Press, 1977.

Cohen, Margaret, *Profane Illumination: Walter Benjamin and the Paris of the Surrealist Revolution*. Berkeley: University of California Press, 1995.

Jarvis, Simon, *Adorno: A Critical Introduction*. Cambridge: Polity, 1998.

Jay, Martin, *Adorno*. London: Fontana, 1984.

Lukács, Georg, *The Lukács Reader*. Ed. Arpad Kadarky. Oxford: Blackwell, 1995.

Lunn, Eugene, *Marxism and Modernism: An Historical Study of Lukacs, Brecht, Benjamin and Adorno*. Berkeley: University of California Press, 1982.

Marcus, Laura and Lynda Neal (eds), *The Actuality of Walter Benjamin*. New Formations No. 20. London: Lawrence and Wishart, 1993.

Pensky, Max, *Melancholy Dialectics: Walter Benjamin and the Play of Mourning*. Amherst: University of Massachusetts Press, 1993.

Roberts, Julian, *Walter Benjamin*. London: Macmillan, 1982.

Rose, Gillian, *The Melancholy Science: An Introduction to the Thought of Theodor W. Adorno*. London: Macmillan, 1978.

Smith, Gary (ed.), *Benjamin: Philosophy, Aesthetics, History*. Chicago: University of Chicago Press, 1990.

Tar, Zoltan, *The Frankfurt School: The Critical Theories of Max Horkheimer and Theodor W. Adorno*. Foreword Michael Landmann. New York: John Wiley, 1977.

Wiggershaus, Rolf, *The Frankfurt School: Its History, Theories and Political Significance*. Trans. Michael Robertson. Cambridge: Polity, 1994.

Wolin, Richard, *Walter Benjamin: An Aesthetic of Redemption*. 1982. Berkeley: University of California Press, 1994.

CHAPTER 10   POSTSTRUCTURALISM

Cohen, Tom (ed.), *Jacques Derrida and the Humanities: A Critical Reader*. Cambridge: Cambridge University Press, 2002.

Culler, Jonathan, *The Pursuit of Signs: Semiotics, Literature, Deconstruction*. London: Routledge and Kegan Paul, 1981.

Derrida, Jacques, *A Derrida Reader: Between the Blinds*. Ed. Peggy Kamuf. New York: Columbia University Press, 1991.

Derrida, Jacques, *Dissemination*. 1972. Trans. Barbara Johnson. London: Athlone Press, 1981.

Derrida, Jacques, *Margins of Philosophy*. 1972. Trans. and additional notes Alan Bass. Brighton: Harvester Press, 1982.

Derrida, Jacques, *Of Grammatology*. 1967. Trans. Gayatri Chakrovorty Spivak. Baltimore and London: Johns Hopkins University Press, 1976.

Derrida, Jacques, *Positions*. 1972. Trans. Alan Bass. London: Athlone Press, 1981.

Derrida, Jacques, *Speech and Phenomena and Other Essays on Husserl's Theory of Signs*. 1967. Trans. David Allison. Evanston, IL: Northwestern University Press, 1979.

Derrida, Jacques, *Writing and Difference*. 1967. Trans. Alan Bass. London: Routledge and Kegan Paul, 1978.

Lentricchia, Frank, *After the New Criticism*. London: Athlone Press, 1980.

Norris, Christopher, *Deconstruction: Theory and Practice*. London: Methuen, 1982.

Norris, Christopher, *Derrida*. London: Fontana Press, 1987.

Ryan, Michael, *Marxism and Deconstruction: A Critical Articulation*. Baltimore: Johns Hopkins University Press, 1982.

Wood, David (ed.), *Derrida: A Critical Reader*. Oxford: Blackwell, 1992.

Index